Communicate in French
WRITING

David Morris

Hutchinson

London   Melbourne   Sydney   Auckland   Johannesburg

Hutchinson Education

An imprint of Century Hutchinson Ltd
62–65 Chandos Place, London WC2N 4NW

Century Hutchinson Australia Pty Ltd
16–22 Church Street, Hawthorn, Melbourne, Victoria 3122, Australia

Century Hutchinson New Zealand Ltd
32–34 View Road, PO Box 40-086, Glenfield, Auckland 10, New Zealand

Century Hutchinson South Africa (Pty) Ltd
PO Box 337, Bergvlei 2012, South Africa

First published 1987

Typeset in 12/13 Century Schoolbook
by Hope Services, Abingdon, Oxon

Printed and bound in Great Britain by
Scotprint Ltd., Musselburgh

British Library Cataloguing in Publication Data
Morris, David
Communicate in French writing.
1. French language – Composition and exercises
I. Title
808′.0441′076   PC2420
ISBN 0–09–173081–3

Acknowledgements
The author gratefully acknowledges the help he has received from:
Mrs Jocelyne Varley and Mlle Gladys Guédon, French Assistante, for their
advice on matters French; and pupils at Allerton Grange School, who have,
at various times, tested ideas and acted as guinea pigs.

Photographs by the author.

Note about the author

David Morris is Head of Modern Languages at Allerton Grange High School, Leeds. He is also a member of the Northern Examining Association French Panel for GCSE and has been a member of several working parties developing new examinations. As well as being National Assistant Honorary Secretary of the Modern Language Association, he is Honorary Secretary of its Yorkshire Branch. With Alan Smalley, he is co-author of *The MLA Modern Language Teachers' Handbook*, published by Hutchinson.

TO CYNTHIA

Contents

Unit 7 Writing stories and essays   [HIGHER]

A Writing stories from an outline

B Continuing stories

C Writing picture stories

Unit 8 Games and puzzles

Topic Index   112

Introduction

To the teacher

Communicate in French: Writing is intended for pupils sitting for the GCSE examination. It provides systematic practice in the skill of writing, in accordance with the ground rules laid down by the National Criteria.

These National Criteria were published in 1985 after prolonged consultations with teachers of modern languages, language associations and others with a professional interest in the teaching, learning and using of modern languages.

The most important areas to stress in these criteria as they affect the skill of writing are as follows:

1 Work, exercises and tests must foster **practical communication**.
2 These tasks must be based on **authentic** material.
3 They must form a sound base for work beyond the classroom.
4 They must provide enjoyment and intellectual stimulation.
5 They must foster positive attitudes to France and the French.

All the examining groups have published their syllabuses for French, and there is a remarkable similarity in the range of tests available. **Communicate in French: Writing** provides a systematic coverage of all the types of tests envisaged in this new examination based on realistic and authentic material.

Syllabuses produced by the examining groups are all described in terms of functions and notions, settings and topics, and are all circumscribed by a vocabulary list.

1

Thus the days of the 'secret garden' of the syllabus are over and teachers can now be certain what tasks their pupils will be asked to perform in the examination.

Used in conjunction with the other titles in the 'Communicate in French' series, this book will provide more than enough practice for pupils who will enter for both **Basic** and **Higher** level tests.

The new emphasis on communication also brings with it the need for a fresh approach to assessment. Assessment of pupils' work should emphasize positive communication and how well the pupil has carried out the task set. This does not imply native-speaker competence, as it must be assumed that the pupil is not French. Nor does it imply that accuracy can be thrown to the wind – lack of accuracy may very well impede comprehension and the successful completion of the communicative activity. Teachers marking the exercises in this book should bear these points in mind.

This book is divided into several sections, each one covering a different type of writing activity. The exemplar material is followed by a series of tasks for the pupils to dip into according to their needs and in conjunction with their usual class textbook.

Tasks at both **Basic** and **Higher** levels in this new examination must be worthwhile and in no way trivial. It is hoped that all pupils will find all tasks in this book both useful and interesting. The examination syllabuses do not include the writing skill in the common core, but teachers should note that an attempt at basic writing is essential for pupils hoping to gain a Grade C or better. **Basic** papers involve the possibility of writing lists, short messages, postcards, form-filling and a 'friendly' letter. More complicated letters and story-telling are reserved for the **Higher** level. Thus each section of this book can be used according to the examination scheme for the individual board, and teachers should refer to their particular syllabus.

It is also to be hoped that pupils will enjoy learning French. If they do not, then we are making things unnecessarily difficult. To that end, this book also contains a few ideas for games and puzzles. We hope that this will stimulate you to be inventive yourself.

Note: When counting words as part of the assessment of pupils' work, the examination boards set their own criteria, but teachers may find the following guidelines useful.

A 'word' may be defined as what appears between two 'spaces'. Thus *il y a* is three words, *il n'y a pas* is four and *porte-clés* is one. It is arbitrary, but consistent.

To the pupil

Communicate in French: Writing is designed to give you practice in the various writing tasks you may be faced with in the GCSE examination. It is divided into various sections which cover all that you will need at both **Basic** and **Higher** levels. Learning to write in French can be both useful and enjoyable, so the tasks you will be asked to do are valuable in the context of your visiting France or French-speaking countries, or receiving a French-speaking visitor here.

Basic level may involve you in writing lists, messages, postcards, filling in forms and writing simple letters. At **Higher** level you will be asked to write a more complex letter and an account or description. Check with your teacher exactly what **your** examination will involve.

If you work through this book in conjunction with your teacher (or on your own) you will be able to face the examination with a great deal of confidence.

Each section has some tips and hints to help you complete the task successfully. However, there are some general rules which, if considered carefully, will help you face the French examination calmly.

3

1 Read all the instructions on the paper carefully – even if you **think** you know what they say.
2 Plan your time according to the number of questions to be answered.
3 Check the number of questions to be answered – and answer only the required number.
4 Check for the number of words you are asked to write. Keep to that number as closely as you can. Too few words may lead to a loss of marks. Too many words are a waste of time and lead to errors.
5 Look for clues in the titles and the context of the questions – these are valuable.
6 Use the French you know – don't invent!
7 Try to complete every part of the question. Don't leave gaps.
8 Check your work systematically and make sure that it is neat – this makes a good impression.

Enjoy yourself and *bonne chance*!

Unit 1 *WRITING LISTS*

You often need to write a list to help you remember important things. You may be going shopping, for example, planning a journey, packing your suitcase for a holiday in France, or planning a party. You may want to leave a list for someone else to consult.

In this section you will be asked to complete all kinds of lists, such as you may find you need in France or if you have a French visitor at home here in Britain.

Copy these lists into your exercise book – please don't write in this book!

1 Some French schoolchildren have been staying with families in your area as part of an exchange visit arranged by your school. After their departure, it is discovered that some of the visitors have left things behind.

You are asked by your teacher to complete a list of all the articles to send to the French school. Write out, in French, a list of eight different articles. Mention where and when each article was found. The first is done for you – a red woollen pullover was found at school on Thursday.

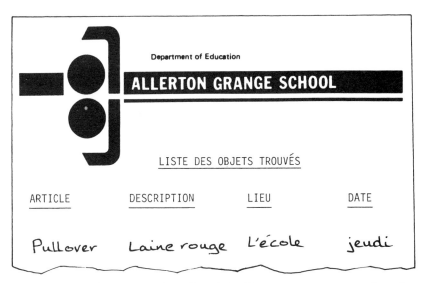

Department of Education

ALLERTON GRANGE SCHOOL

LISTE DES OBJETS TROUVÉS

ARTICLE	DESCRIPTION	LIEU	DATE
Pullover	Laine rouge	L'école	jeudi

2 During the French schoolchildren's visit, you decide one Saturday to go on a picnic with your French guest and your sister. Your guest offers to do the shopping, but his English is not very good. You therefore write out a shopping list for him in French.

Write out, in French, a list of items (both food and drink) that you will need for the picnic. Indicate the shop where they can be bought (there is no supermarket in your area). The first one is done for you – now write eight other items.

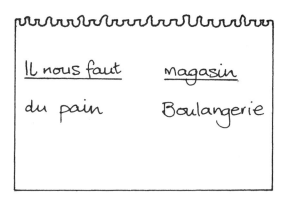

Il nous faut   magasin

du pain   Boulangerie

3 On your return visit to France, you find out one Sunday that today is your friend's sister's birthday. You decide to throw a party.

Write out, in French, a list of items you will need for a surprise buffet meal. It is Sunday morning in Amboise – the local shops are open, but the supermarket is closed. The first item is done for you – now write ten more.

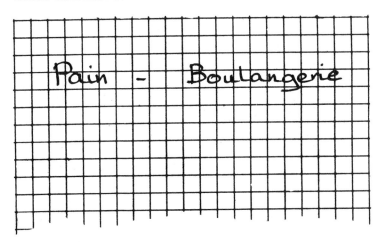

4 During your two-week stay in France, you want to buy presents for your family, relatives and closest friends at school. It would be bad if you missed someone out, so you decide to write out a list in French and discuss your ideas with your penfriend's family.

Here are the people you must buy presents for: mother, father, sister (older), brother (younger), grandmother, grandfather, your best friends at school (one boy and one girl).

Write a list, in French, of the eight different souvenirs you hope to buy. The first one is done for you.

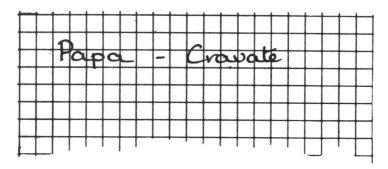

5 Unfortunately, on your journey to France, you lose your suitcase. Before you go to the station to see if it has turned up, you write a list, in French, of the major contents so that they will be fresh in your mind if you have to report the loss.

If you are a boy, you might start your list like this:

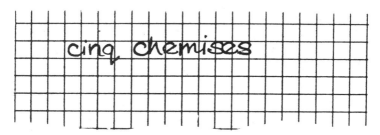

If you are a girl, your list might begin like this:

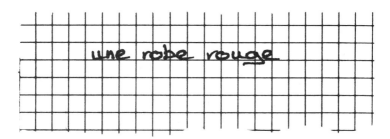

Now write, in French, ten more things that you brought with you.

6 You are staying in France in a flat which your family has rented. Unfortunately, while you are out one day, a robbery takes place and several things are stolen from your bedroom.

Look at the two pictures below and decide what is missing.

Make a list of everything that has been taken so that you can give it to the police when they arrive to make enquiries. Write the list in French of course, since you are in France!

7 Your family owns a cottage in the Yorkshire Dales. This year the family of your French penfriend are coming to spend two weeks there. They have not been to England before, and you make sure that there is some food in the cottage for their arrival.

Write a message, in French, telling them that they will find five essential foods in the fridge and five other food items in the larder, or kitchen cupboard. The message has been started for you. Copy it into your exercise book, then add the names of the other foods.

j'ai laissé dans le frigo : du beurre

et dans la cuisine il y a :

des pommes de terre

Bon Séjour
Paul.

8 One year, you invite your French penfriend to stay with you during the summer in a cottage that your family has rented. Everyone must share in the chores – your mother doesn't want to do all the work!

Here are a few of the tasks that have to be done during the week:

Do the shopping	Tidy your room
Wash up	Clear the table
Make the beds	Take the dog for a walk
Clean the car	Prepare sandwiches for
Prepare the breakfast	picnic

Your mother puts up a rota in the kitchen so that everyone knows what they have to do. She asks you to make a similar list in French for Marcel to consult.

The list has been started for you. Copy it into your exercise book then complete it, in French. (Each task must be different!)

	Peter	Marcel
Lundi :	faire la vaisselle	
mardi :		
mercredi :		débarrasser la table
jeudi :		
vendredi :	promener le chien	
samedi :		
dimanche :		Fin de séjour !

11

9 Your French penfriend is coming to visit you soon. You decide to send him/her a letter outlining your plans for visits, excursions and activities during his/her stay. You include in your letter a section of a diary, setting out some possibilities.

Some suggestions are already marked in. Copy the diary extract into your exercise book then add eight other suggestions to suit you and your visitor. Write them in French so that your friend's family will understand.

You won't want a full day of outings every day, but you might like to include, for example, a visit to the swimming pool, to the cinema or to a disco, or a game of tennis.

	MATIN	APRÈS-MIDI
3 Sunday dimanche		
4 Monday lundi		Visite au musée
5 Tuesday mardi		
6 Wednesday mercredi		
7 Thursday jeudi		
8 Friday vendredi		
9 Saturday samedi	promenade en vélo	

10 You are on holiday in France, staying at a *gîte*. As always, when you arrive you will sign an inventory or list of the equipment provided. Unfortunately there seems to be a page missing from the list – the one describing the contents of the kitchen.

You decide to add a page of your own, listing the kitchen's contents. The list has been started for you. Copy it into your exercise book then complete it by adding, in French, seven other items and their quantities. (Do not include 'fixed' items such as the cooker or washing machine.)

SASSAY

N° 121 - 2 EPIS
Capacité maximum 4 personnes.

Vieille maison, style local, située sur une exploitation agricole, indépendante avec terrain attenant.
— Séjour avec coin cuisine (cheminée) ; 1 chambre (1 lit de 2 personnes, 1 lit d'enfant) ; 1 chambre (2 lits de 1 personne) ; salle d'eau, W.C.
Chauffage électrique.
Animaux non admis.
Barbecue, portique, vente de fromages de chèvre, vin, fruits et légumes.

Prix par semaine			Week-end (2 nuits)
Hors saison	Juin-Sept. Vac. scol.	Juill./ Août	
345 F	480 F	635 F	250 F

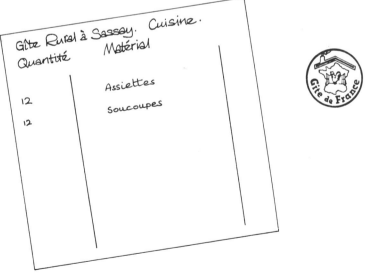

Gîte Rural à Sassay. Cuisine.
Quantité   Matériel

              Assiettes
12
              Soucoupes
12

11 During the school year, your penfriend asks you to send him/her details of your school timetable for use in a project he/she has to do.

This is an extract from what you send. Copy the grid into your exercise book then fill in, in French, your subjects and homework.

										Devoirs
lundi										
mardi										
mercredi										
jeudi										
vendredi										

12 While in France you notice a competition on the 'Young Readers' page of the local newspaper. There are various prizes offered, so you decide to enter. Today's competition is a sort of 'I Spy' game. It asks you to identify various signs you may see at the railway station.

Copy the entry form into your exercise book then complete it, in French.

Add your name and French telephone number in the spaces provided.

Concours – SNCF

✗	🚶 ....
🔋	📞 ....
ℹ	🚂→ ....
🚭	**P** ....
🚺	☕ ....

Nom............................ Adresse............................
Téléphone........................ ....

13 You have received a letter from your penfriend in France asking for some information for a project he/she has to do on 'likes and dislikes'. You are asked to fill in, in French, a form he/she has enclosed.

Some things have already been filled in. Copy the form into your exercise book then add, in French, eight other items.

Nom........................ Age........................
J'aime énormément *faire la grasse matinée*
....
....
J'aime assez *écouter la musique classique*
....
....
Je n'aime pas *passer des examens*
....

Merci!

(You could use this topic for a class discussion in your own French class.)

15

14 At the end of your school holiday in France, your teacher asks you and your friends to write a list of all the things you bought during your stay, so that it will be easier to pass through Customs.

Write a list, in French, of ten items that you have purchased during your stay. These can be presents, souvenirs or just things for yourself.

15 While you are on a camping holiday in France at the *Parc de Fierbois* in the Loire Valley, you see that there are various competitions (and prizes!) for young campers. One of the competitions is a sort of 'I Spy' and you decide to answer.

You have to decide what the following ten signs mean. Write your list in French to hand in at the camp office and beat the French at their own game!

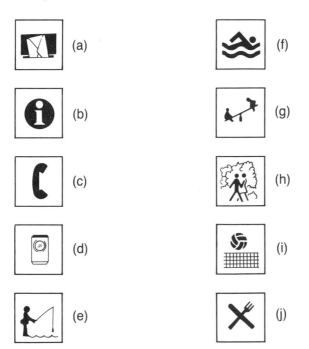

(a)

(b)

(c)

(d)

(e)

(f)

(g)

(h)

(i)

(j)

16 Your French penfriend has asked you to help in a survey he/she is doing at his school. He/she thought it would be interesting to find out what sports are popular in Britain as compared to France. You think it is a good topic for discussion in your own French class!

Your penfriend has sent you a collection of 'pin-drawing' sportsmen. First you must write the name of each activity in French. The first one is done for you.

Now write the list in order of preference – the most popular first.

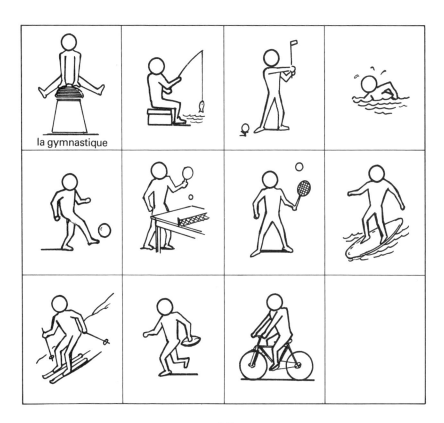

Unit 2   WRITING SHORT MESSAGES

Writing a message is a **Basic** task, but it is a very useful task in all sorts of circumstances. You may have to leave a message for a French-speaking person while you are in France or when you have a French visitor at your home in Britain.

Usually, a message will be very brief (ask your teacher how many words you should write). It is important, however, that you write clearly and in the best French possible so that the message will be understood. The message should be short and to the point but don't forget that you should still put *le/la/les/un/une* etc. in front of nouns and not leave out such words as we often do in English.

Here is an example:

You are staying in France at the home of your penfriend. It is near the end of your two-week stay. Your friend has gone to the dentist, and you decide to go into the town to do some last-minute shopping for presents to take home to your family. You need to let your friend know where you have gone and that you expect to be back after five in time for the evening meal.

18

You would write something like this:

> Je me suis absenté pour
> acheter des cadeaux.
> Je passerai l'après-midi en ville.
> Serai de retour probablement
> après 5h 90, mais je prendrai le
> souper avec toi.

Now try writing the following messages for yourself. Normally thirty words should be enough. Write all the messages in French and be as accurate as you can.

1 Your friend has gone out. While he is away, the telephone rings.

Write a short message, in French, to explain:
a) Who telephoned.
b) That the football match begins at 2 p.m. in the park.
c) That your friend must be at the café by 1.30 p.m.

2 Your penfriend's mother has offered to do some shopping for you while you are at the cinema.

Write a short note, in French, to ask her:
a) To buy you two postcards to send to England.
b) To buy two stamps for these postcards and also four stamps for letters to England.
c) Say that you have left a fifty-franc note on the table in your bedroom.

3 You are in France with your family and are staying at a hotel in Le Mont-Dore. You are expecting a French friend to call in to see you, as he is in the area also. The problem is that you do not know at what time he will arrive.

Write a note (in French) for the hotel receptionist, so that he/she knows what to do when your friend arrives.
a) Say that your friend is called Nicolas Menet and he lives in Lille.
b) You will be at the swimming pool all morning.
c) You would like your friend to have lunch with you in the restaurant.

4 While you are staying with your penfriend, the telephone rings.

Take down (in French) the following message which turns out to be for her father:
a) The Garage Jarrier rang at 10 a.m.
b) The car is now ready.
c) The repair will cost 600 francs.
d) The garage is closed tomorrow (Saturday).

5   While your penfriend is out, the telephone rings. It is Marie-Claire, who wants to leave a message.

Write the message in French:
a) Marie-Claire telephoned at 2.30 p.m.
b) She thanks you for the invitation to the party.
c) She will come tomorrow at 8 p.m.
d) She will bring some cakes and lemonade.

6   The telephone is really busy! A little later it rings again. This time it is your penfriend's aunt.

Write the following message in French:
a) Aunt Martine rang.
b) She thanks you for her birthday presents.
c) She thought the chocolates were delicious and she liked the flowers.
d) She will write a letter this weekend.

7   Unfortunately, while staying at your friend's house in France, you have a little accident! Your friend isn't in at the time and you wish to leave a message for his/her parents to read on their return from work.

Write the following message in French:
a) You dropped a bottle of wine on the floor and broke it.
b) You are sorry and you have cleaned the floor.
c) You have gone to buy a new bottle.

8   One day, while you are in France, you feel unwell. It is not serious, but you decide to go to bed. The family have gone out for an hour to visit a relative.

Leave a message for them, in French, so that they will not be worried on their return.
a) Say you feel ill: you have a headache and tummy-ache.
b) You took an aspirin and drank some mineral water from the fridge.
c) You went to bed at 8 p.m.

21

9 Your birthday falls on 10th August, while you are in France. Your host family is going to arrange a party for you! You decide to write all the invitations in French.

Each card should contain the following information:
a) The reason for the party.
b) Where and when it will take place.
c) Ask for everyone to bring records to dance to.
d) State the finishing time.
(Begin your invitation: *On t'invite . . .*)

On t'invite

10 Your visit to France is almost over. However, you have forgotten the return train times. You telephone the local station and the taxi.

Write a note in French for your hosts so that they know the details.
a) Your train will leave the central station at 10.05 a.m.
b) You have telephoned for a taxi for Friday morning.
c) It will arrive here at 9.30 a.m.
d) You will get up at 7.30 a.m.

11 One day, while your French friend is on a return visit to you in Britain, he/she sleeps late, after a very late night. You have to go out and so you leave a message for him/her.

As his/her English is poor, you write it in French. Say the following:
a) You have gone to the dentist at 10 a.m.
b) You will meet him/her at the station at 11 a.m.
c) He/she must take bus number 14 and get off at the town hall.

12 While this friend is staying at your house, he/she always seems to get lost. To make sure he/she manages to find the station, you decide to leave a sketch-map with directions from your house to the station.

Using the rough map on page 24 to help you, write the message in French to give the necessary instructions (leave house, turn left, turn right after cinema, first left, cross market square, etc.).

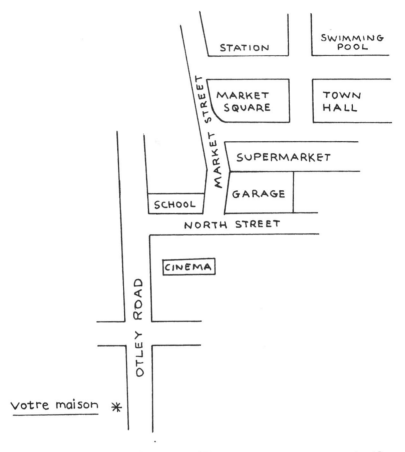

STATION

SWIMMING POOL

MARKET STREET

MARKET SQUARE

TOWN HALL

MARKET STREET

SUPERMARKET

GARAGE

SCHOOL

NORTH STREET

CINEMA

A ROAD

OTLEY ROAD

votre maison ✳

13 While on holiday in France, you stay at the Camping du Beaujolais. You know that your French friend is staying at the Ibis Hotel nearby. However, when you call, he/she isn't there. The hotel provides some paper for you to leave a message.

Copy the form into your exercise book. Fill in the top half as appropriate and then write the following message in French:

a) You will telephone this evening.

b) You are staying at the Camping du Beaujolais.

c) You will be there until Wednesday.

DIJON

DESTINATAIRE ....

APPT. N° ....

DATE .... HEURE...............................

PENDANT VOTRE ABSENCE

M ....

DE ....

N° ....

- ☐ a téléphoné
- ☑ est venu vous voir
- ☐ désire un rendez-vous

- ☐ demande que vous le rappeliez
- ☐ vous rappellera
- ☐ vous a rappelé

MESSAGE

....

....

....

....

VISA :

IMPRIMERIE CAILLET — 14, RUE COLONEL-MOLL, 21100 DIJON — ☎ (80) 55 37 63

14 While in France, you and your penfriend decide to visit a local château. Your friend goes to the bus station to find out the times of the buses and you go to the Tourist Office to find details of the château.

Write notes, in French, from the information you obtain. Your notes should contain the following details:

a) The château at Chenonceau opens at 9 a.m. and closes at 7 p.m.
b) The cost of entry is 20 francs but there is half-price for under-15s.
c) It is open every day in August.

15 While in France, you receive an invitation to a party. It is from a neighbour, but you are unable to accept because your host family has arranged to take you away for the weekend.

Write a short note, in French, which you will leave for the neighbour.
a) Thank him/her for the kind invitation.
b) Say that you are sorry, but you cannot accept.
c) You are going to Blois for the weekend with your penfriend and his/her family.
d) You will call in on Monday.

16 While in France, you go to visit some friends. On returning to your hotel, you discover that you have left your wallet at their house. You telephone, but get no reply. You return to their house, but there is no one in. You decide to leave a note.

Write the following message in French:
a) You have left your wallet in the house.
b) It is in the garden where you ate or in the lounge where you watched TV.
c) You will call round tomorrow morning, or they can telephone you on 36 64 91 23.

17 While your French friend is out, the telephone rings. It is the hairdressing salon. The receptionist asks you to give your friend a message.

Write the message in French.
a) The hairdresser is ill.
b) He wants to change your friend's appointment.
c) The new time is Saturday at 10.30 a.m.
d) Will your friend telephone and let them know if that is all right.

27

18 While you are staying in Lille with your friend, you go into the city centre one day. You arrange to meet your friend's father at 4 p.m. at the car which has been left in a car park.

When you arrive, he is not there. You decide to explore a little more and in order not to cause any worry, you leave a note tucked under the windscreen wipers of the car.

Write the note in French. Say the following:
a) You are going to the record shop and bookshop in the Grande Place.
b) Tell him not to wait.
c) You will return by bus to their house.
d) You will be back before 6 p.m.

Unit 3 *WRITING POSTCARDS AND SIMILAR MESSAGES*

[BASIC]

We all like to have a postcard from family or friends who are on holiday. Your French friends would certainly appreciate you sending them a postcard while you are away, so here is the chance to practise!

It is also polite to send a thank you note to someone after a nice evening out, after a party or receiving a present. Have you noticed how many shops now sell special thank you cards? Even the French are now doing this sort of thing. There are some ideas for practising thank you notes in this section.

Remember to write your note or message as clearly and accurately as possible – it leaves a good impression. Ask your teacher how many words to write – it will be between twenty-five and thirty.

A Postcards and short messages

1 Imagine that you have just received this postcard from a friend who is on holiday in La Rochelle.

Now send a postcard to your French friend (written in French, of course) from your holiday in Scarborough.

a) Say that you are staying in a hotel in Scarborough.

LA ROCHELLE (Charente - Maritime)
Le vieux Port
Tour St Nicolas et tour de la Chaîne.

Édition de Luxe

Cher Peter,

Mon premier jour à la Rochelle et je trouve cela fantastique ! Andrew et Ewan se prennent déjà pour les rois du camp. Il fait très chaud et nous nageons à la mer tous les jours. Le soir, nous racontons des histoires assis autour d'un grand feu. Jaloux, non ?

Jean

Peter KinG
26 St Anne's Road
LEEDS 6
GRANDE - BRETAGNE

Reproduction interdite - Imprimé en Espagne

Photo Editions BOS 46400 St. Céré Tél. (65) 38 13 17

b) You are with your family, and the weather is warm.
c) You go to the swimming pool every day and to the cinema or theatre in the evening.
d) Wish your friend a happy holiday.

POST Bamforth CARD
B & Co. LTD

POST OFFICE
PREFERRED
40a

'COLOR GLOSS' VIEW SERIES
PUBLISHED BY BAMFORTH & CO. LTD. HOLMFIRTH. YORKSHIRE

Castle and Bay
North Bay - Peasholm Park
The Harbour

— REPRODUCED FROM A COLOUR PHOTOGRAPH —

SCARBOROUGH

2 Your French friend lives in Poitiers. This postcard was sent from La Rochelle on the Atlantic coast, where she spent a day. As you will see, she went there with some friends and had a splendid time.

En Aunis
171-82 - LA ROCHELLE (Charente-Maritime)
Le port, les Tours St Nicolas et de
la Chaîne.

Chère Pauline,
Après deux heures et demi
de train, je suis arrivée à
la Rochelle à 10 heures.
Il fait très beau. J'ai
visité les magasins et j'ai
acheté des souvenirs.
Je finirai la journée au
port. Il est magnifique.
Les bateaux aussi!
A bientôt j'espère. Claire

Pauline SMITH

5 Holt Lane

LEEDS 16

GRANDE - BRETAGNE.

Now send a postcard to your French friend (written in French, of course), describing your weekend in Scarborough.
a) You are staying in the Youth Hostel.
b) You have made a visit to the castle and it was boring.
c) On Sunday you are going for a bicycle ride.
d) Mention one other thing that you have done.

The Spa Bridge and New Valley Development, Scarborough.   32.

3 Your penfriend sends you a postcard a few days before he is due to arrive in your town for a short stay with you. On the postcard overleaf are details of the place and time of arrival as well as some details to allow you to recognize your friend.

Now write a similar postcard, in French, to your friend in Paris.
a) Say that you will arrive at the Gare du Nord at 5 p.m. (use the 24-hour clock to avoid confusion).
b) You will wait at the Lost Property Office.
c) You will wear an anorak and you have fair hair.
d) You are tall and will carry an English newspaper and a rucksack.

33

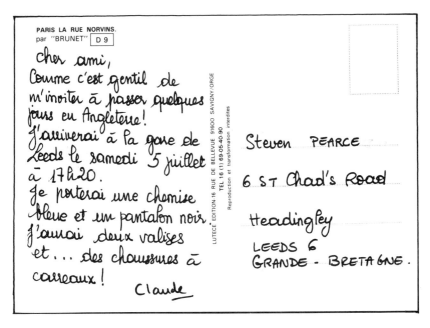

PARIS LA RUE NORVINS.
par "BRUNET" D 9

Cher ami,
Comme c'est gentil de
m'inviter à passer quelques
jours en Angleterre!
J'arriverai à la gare de
Leeds le samedi 5 juillet
à 17h20.
Je porterai une chemise
bleue et un pantalon noir
j'aurai deux valises
et... des chaussures à
carreaux!
                    Claude

Steven   PEARCE

6 ST Chad's Road

Headingley

LEEDS 6
GRANDE - BRETAGNE.

4 Write a postcard, in French, to your French friend.
   a) You are in London and are spending a week in a
      Youth Hostel with a school group as part of your
      History/Geography course.
   b) You eat in the hostel restaurant in the evening,
      but have sandwiches and fruit juice at lunchtime.
   c) The excursions are interesting and you liked the
      visit to the zoo.

5 You have just been to France for two weeks. On
   returning, you write a postcard, in French, to your
   French friend saying:
   a) You had a good journey back to England.
   b) You arrived on time.
   c) You had a great holiday.
   d) You hope to see him/her in your town next year
      during the summer.

6 Your French penfriend is very fond of music. Last weekend you went to Manchester to a concert. Write a postcard, in French, to tell him/her all about it:

   a) You went to Manchester by train with your friend (invent a name!).
   b) The concert was by (add the name).
   c) The music was excellent and you liked the singer(s).
   d) You will send a programme and a photograph soon.

7 This time your holidays are not fun! Write a postcard, in French, to your friend to say:

   a) You are not enjoying yourself.
   b) There are no young people in the village.
   c) There isn't a cinema or a disco.
   d) There is no bus to the town.

8 You have just moved house. Write a postcard, in French, to your French friend, giving him/her your new address. Add the following details:

   a) The house has two floors and four bedrooms.
   b) There is a large garden.
   c) It is better than the other house and it is ten minutes to school on foot.
   d) You hope your friend will come in the summer.

9 You had an agreement to meet a boy/girl friend on the beach but were unable to be there. You really want to meet him/her and so you leave a note, in French, at the *gîte* where he/she is staying.
   a) Say you are sorry, that you didn't see him/her.
   b) You arrived late because the meal was late.
   c) Ask if you can meet at the weekend – suggest a place and time.

10 While you are in France, it is your friend's birthday. You send a birthday card.

As well as signing the card and wishing him/her Happy Birthday, you write a message (in French) in the card to say:
   a) You are sending a present (for example, a box of chocolates).
   b) Ask him/her to tell you how the day was celebrated.
   c) Ask what else he/she had as presents.
   d) Hope to see him/her soon.

11 Imagine that you are a student in France. You have just found a place to live for the year while you study at the university in Angers.

Write a note, in French, to your French friend inviting him/her to come and see you. You should say the following:
a) Invite him/her to your flat next weekend.
b) Say it is near the university.
c) Say it is in La Rue Paul Fort.
d) The bus stop is *Cité Universitaire*.
e) The flat is next to a baker's shop.

B Thank you notes

It is always nice to be polite, especially when you have enjoyed some activity. It is even nicer for your friend or the family to have such a note in French!

Here are some notes for you to write to express your thanks.

12 You have just celebrated your birthday. Your friend in Strasbourg sent you a present – a book about Alsace with some very nice illustrations.

Write a short thank you note in French to say the following:
a) Thank Valérie for the book – the pictures were really good.

b) You also received some records as a present as well as money.
c) You invited twelve friends for a meal to celebrate.
d) You all listened to records after the meal.

13 You have enjoyed a meal in a French home. Write, in French, to the family to thank them.
a) Say thank you for the meal.
b) Say you liked the meat very much and also the delicious sweet!
c) Ask if you can have the recipe for the sweet. You will try to do it at home for your family.

14 You enjoyed a party while in France. Write, in French, to the host/hostess to thank him/her.
a) Say thank you for the invitation.
b) You liked the food and the drinks.
c) You liked meeting all the other people there.
d) The records were good and you were tired this morning!

15 You enjoyed a weekend at your friend's country house. Write a thank you note to your friend, in French.
a) Say thank you for the invitation.
b) You enjoyed the walk to the lake.
c) You enjoyed playing tennis, but left your racket at the park.
d) Ask your friend to collect it, please.

16 After a stay in France, write a postcard, in French, from your home to your friend's parents to say the following:
a) You had a good journey home.
b) You had a nice holiday in France – thank you.
c) You hope that their son or daughter (your friend – invent a name) will be able to come to stay with you next summer.

Unit 4 FILLING IN FORMS

[BASIC]

Nobody really likes filling in forms – but it is sometimes a necessity. You may be a visitor to France and still come across all sorts of forms – in a hotel or campsite, in a supermarket, or even in a restaurant. Sometimes you are obliged to fill them in, and on other occasions you may be asked to do so, in a kind of opinion survey. Also, it does happen that when booking things, even from Britain, the form you have to fill in may be in French.

Here is a selection of real forms for you to fill in. Please don't write in this book – copy the forms into your exercise book, then fill them in.

1   The first example, a hotel registration form, is very easy, since there is help in three languages on the form. It used to be compulsory for all visitors to fill in a form like this on arrival at a hotel. These forms were used by the police as a check (if you have read the novel *The Day of the Jackal* you will know about this).

Today, only a few hotels ask you to fill in this type of form, but you may very well be asked for similar details on a form supplied by the hotel. You should read the instructions carefully and write in block letters except for your signature.

FICHE DE VOYAGEUR	Nom et adresse de l'hôtel
CH. N°	

NOM :_____
Name in capital letters   (écrire en majuscules)
Name (in Druckschrift)

Nom de jeune fille :_____
Maiden name
Mädchen Name

Prénoms :_____
Christian names
Vorname

Né le :_____ à _____
Date and place of birth
Geburtsort - Datum

Département :_____
(ou pays pour l'étranger)
Country - Für Ausländer Angabe des Geburtslandes

Profession :_____
Occupation
Beruf

Domicile habituel :_____
Permanent address
Gewöhnlicher Wohnort

NATIONALITÉ :
Nationality
Nationalität

T. S. V. P.   (Please turn over - Bitte we

Nombre d'enfants de moins de 15 ans accompagnant le chef de

famille :_____
Accompanying children under 15
Zahl der Kinder unter 15 Jahren die den Familienvorstand begleiten

PIÈCE D'IDENTITÉ PRODUITE

Nature :_____

―――― **Pour les étrangers seulement** ――――
(For aliens only) - (Nur für Ausländer)

CARTE D'IDENTITÉ OU PASSEPORT
CERTIFICATE of IDENTITY or PASSPORT
(cross out word not available)
AUSWEIS - PASS

N°_____délivré le :_____
Issued on - Ausgestellt den

à_____par_____
at   by
In   durch

Date d'entrée en France :_____
Date of arrival in France
Datum der Einreise in Frankreich

_____, le_____

Signature
Unterschrift

© 1619

41

2 Sometimes in hotels and restaurants the management want to find out the opinions of their clients. They wish to know what you think of their service, and your opinions (good or bad!) are valued. Here are some examples for you to copy out and complete.

The first one is easy, as the instructions are in three languages. But there is an incentive. Replies will be put in a lottery and the lucky winner will receive a free stay in one of the hotels in the chain – so fill it in carefully! Write your answers in French.

You chose a chicken dish which is a local speciality and is called *Coq au Riesling*. It was excellent! Other things that impressed you were the good service and the fact that the meal wasn't too expensive.

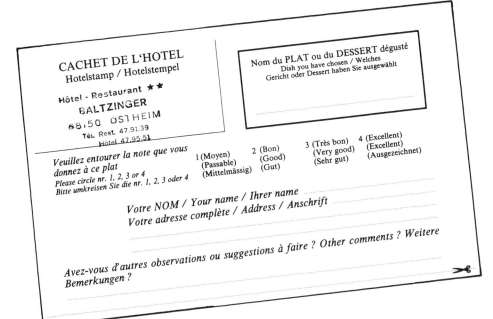

CACHET DE L'HOTEL
Hotelstamp / Hotelstempel

Hôtel - Restaurant ★★
BALTZINGER
68,50 OSTHEIM
Tèl. Rest. 47.91.39
Hôtel 47.95.51

Nom du PLAT ou du DESSERT dégusté
Dish you have chosen / Welches
Gericht oder Dessert haben Sie ausgewählt

*Veuillez entourer la note que vous
donnez à ce plat*
Please circle nr. 1, 2, 3 or 4
Bitte umkreisen Sie die nr. 1, 2, 3 oder 4

1 (Moyen)
(Passable)
(Mittelmässig)

2 (Bon)
(Good)
(Gut)

3 (Très bon)
(Very good)
(Sehr gut)

4 (Excellent)
(Excellent)
(Ausgezeichnet)

Votre NOM / Your name / Ihrer name
Votre adresse complète / Address / Anschrift

*Avez-vous d'autres observations ou suggestions à faire ? Other comments ? Weitere
Bemerkungen ?*

3 This hotel also wants your opinions after your stay – so fill in the form in French and leave it at the reception.

The hotel was called *La Croix Blanche*. The welcome was kind and polite. The service was good, both in the hotel and the restaurant. The room was comfortable and the bathroom was especially clean. You enjoyed your stay there.

LA CROIX BLANCHE

FAITES-NOUS PART DE VOS OBSERVATIONS

En écrivant à M. le Président SCHWOERER
INTER-HOTEL - GD HOTEL - 16, av. Foch
67110 NIEDERBRONN LES BAINS. Tél (88)09.02.60

J'ai séjourné dans l'INTER-HOTEL...........
....

Mes observations sont les suivantes :
....

Accueil : ....
....

Service : ....
....

Équipements : ....
....

4 The *Hotel Campanile* is a chain of motels found all over France. Their form is more complicated but not too difficult to complete. Fill it in in French — the management will value your comments.

This time make up your own comments. Here are some ideas to help you: the hotel is in Le Havre, you were satisfied in every way with the accommodation, food and service.

Vous êtes venu à Campanile, nous vous en remercions. Pour nous aider à rendre votre séjour toujours plus agréable, nous serions heureux que vous acceptiez de répondre à ces quelques questions.

— Hôtel gril Campanile de _____ Date de séjour : _____

— Raisons qui ont motivé votre choix : _____ Motif _____ tourisme-affaire _____

Recommandation ☐   Publicité ☐ _____

Autres _____

— Voulez-vous noter de 1 à 10 : l'hôtel _____ le restaurant gril _____

l'accueil _____ le confort de la chambre _____ le confort des sanitaires _____

le petit déjeuner "buffet" _____ le déjeuner _____ le dîner _____

— Avez-vous utilisé notre "plateau courtoisie" dans la chambre :

Oui ☐   Non ☐   Suggestions : _____

— Avez-vous pris un repas au gril ?

Oui ☐   Non ☐   Remarques : _____

— Avez-vous trouvé les prix en rapport avec la qualité ? :

- de l'hébergement   - de la restauration

Oui ☐   Non ☐   Oui ☐   Non ☐

Suggestions _____

— Comment jugez-vous ces formules d'hébergement et de restauration _____

_____

_____

— Si vous le souhaitez, indiquez : Votre nom, votre adresse et votre profession.

Nom : _____

Adresse : _____

Profession : _____

---

5 Many areas in France have special services, run by the Tourist Office, to help you book a holiday in a *gîte*, a hotel or a holiday centre. At the back of the brochure you will find a booking form such as the one opposite. You are the only person in your family who can read and write French, so you must complete the booking form for a two-week stay in a *gîte* in the town of Blois in the Loire Valley. (Make up dates.)

The cost for the two weeks will be 1,200 francs and the *gîte* is called *Beau Rivage*. All other details will be personal to your family.

44

Remember to include your mother and father and any brothers or sisters you may have. The reference number is Y149.

---

fiche de demande de réservation

à nous adresser dûment complétée, après vous être assuré auprès de notre service, de l'état des disponibilités de la formule que vous avez choisie. Merci.

Nom :

Prénom :

Adresse précise :

Code postal :   Ville :

Téléphone personnel :   professionnel :

Profession (facultatif) :

Nombre total de participants :
dont adultes (+ 18 ans) :
dont enfants (précisez l'âge) :

Venez-vous avec des animaux ?
Si oui, précisez :

Référence du séjour :

Dates du séjour :

Coût du séjour :

Ayant pris connaissance des Conditions Générales de vente
JE JOINS LE MONTANT DE L'ACOMPTE DE 25 % soit

.... F

Banque :   solde à régler
Numéro du chèque :   1 mois avant l'arrivée

Fait à   , le   Signature :

A RETOURNER A : TOURISME EN LOIR-ET-CHER
11, place du Château - 41000 BLOIS
Tél. (54) 78.55.50 - Télex 751375 LC TOUR

Groupement d'Intérêt économique, régi par l'ordonnance du 23 septembre

- ✄ - -

COMMENT AVEZ-VOUS EU CONNAISSANCE DE CETTE BROCHURE ?

☐ Par l'Office de Tourisme de BLOIS
☐ Par un syndicat d'initiative, lequel ?
☐ Par un article paru dans la presse
☐ Par des amis
☐ Autre.

6 Let's hope that it doesn't happen to you, but we all lose things at times. If you lose something in France, you should report the loss to the police. You will probably be asked to fill in a form similar to the one below.

```
        SERVICE DES OBJETS TROUVES.


    LIEU DE LA PERTE (1)
Dans le métro  (ligne No      )
Dans l'autobus  (ligne No.      )
Dans un taxi
Sur la voie publique
Dans un établissement public

NOM: ...................................... M., Mme., Mlle.,
DEMEURANT.................................................
TELEPHONE.................
PROFESSION................

PARIS.................... LE........................

SIGNATURE...........................................

DATE DE LA PERTE............. HEURE....................
        OBJET PERDU.
QU'AVEZ-VOUS PERDU? ....................................

        DESCRIPTION.
1. FORME, COULEUR.........................................
   ......................................................
   ......................................................
2. CONTENU...............................................
   ......................................................
   ......................................................
3. AUTRES DETAILS .......................................
   ......................................................
   ......................................................
4. VALEUR DE L'OBJET.....................................

Nota: (1) A préciser.
```

46

Copy and complete the form in French for two incidents:
a) Naming the objects shown in the picture of the suitcase.
b) Naming the objects shown in the picture of the briefcase.

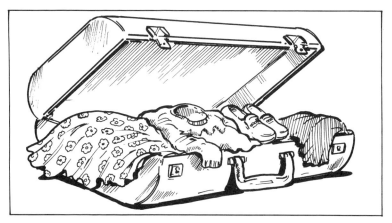

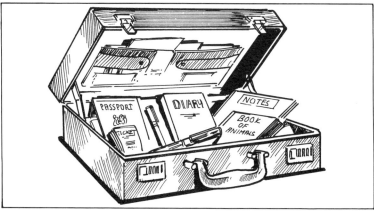

On both occasions you lost your valuables on the underground in Paris (on Line One between the station at *Charles de Gaulle-Etoile* and the station at the *Louvre*). It was late afternoon on Monday 3rd August.

7 You are hoping to go on a school exchange and stay with a French family for two weeks. The teacher in your 'twin' school sends you a form to fill in. This asks for information about yourself in order that you may be given a suitable partner, with similar likes and dislikes, interests and family situation.

Copy the form then fill in the details in French.

```
           LYCEE JEAN PERRIN - LAMBERSART.
              ECHANGES SCOLAIRES 19    .
                 Fiche d'inscription.


    NOM..................... PRENOMS..........................

    ADRESSE.....................................,...................

    CODE POSTALE......................... TELEPHONE.............

    AGE ................ANS .............MOIS.

    AVEZ-VOUS DES FRERES?................ DES SOEURS?.............
    LEURS AGES......................................................

    PROFESSION  DES PARENTS .......................................

    AVEZ-VOUS DES ANIMAUX A LA MAISON? ............................

    LESQUELS? .....................................................

    L'ECOLE.  DANS QUELLE CLASSE ETES-VOUS? ...................

    MATIERES ETUDIEES .............................................

    ...............................................................

    LANGUES PARLEES ...............................................

    INTERETS ......................................................

    ...............................................................

    SANTE .........................................................

    DETAILS DE LA MAISON. NOMBRE DE CHAMBRES ....................

    LE CORRESPONDANT / LA CORRESPONDANDANTE AURA/UNE CHAMBRE A PART /
    UN LIT DANS VOTRE CHAMBRE?  (Rayer la mention inutile)
    EST-CE QU'IL Y A UNE VOITURE A LA MAISON? ...................
    ACTIVITES PROPOSEES PENDANT LE SEJOUR ......................
    ...............................................................
    SIGNE. ..................          DATE...................
```

You can still send a message by telegram in France. It can be very useful on occasions, especially if there is no telephone.

Don't forget that you pay for each word of the message you write, but at the same time the message must be understandable to the other person. In the example below you can see the sort of form you will have to fill in at the post office. You fill in the section within the thick line only – the rest is for the post office officials.

Now study the example:

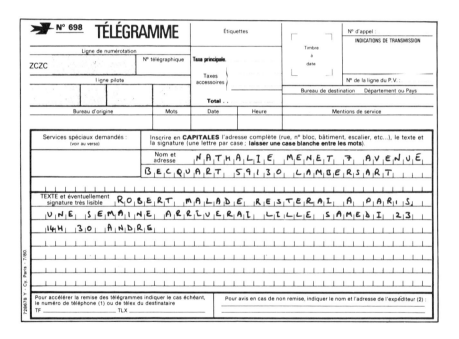

Imagine that you are in France and wish to send the following messages (in French, of course) to friends there. Write the name and address of the person to whom the telegram is being sent, then your message.

49

8 While on holiday in France you are on your way to see a friend who has just moved into a new house. Her telephone has not yet been installed. Unfortunately your car breaks down and you are forced to stay over-night in a hotel in Calais.

Send a telegram to explain what has happened and that you now expect to reach her house on Sunday at about 2 p.m. Don't forget to put your name at the end.

The address is: Régine Kiczanski, Allée des Haies, Duisans, 62100.

9 After visiting your friend's house, you discover that you have left your camera there. Send her a telegram, asking for your camera to be sent to your home address. Say that you will pay all the postage costs.

Don't forget to include your home address or to put your name at the end.

10 There is a train strike in France and so you are unable to continue your journey by train as planned. You are due to travel from Paris to Biarritz to stay with friends in their seaside flat.

Write a telegram to Nicolas Menet, Résidence des Pins, Biarritz, 64100, to say that you will fly to Bordeaux airport. Ask him to meet flight *Air Inter 604*, which will arrive at 16.30 today. Explain that the delay is due to the rail strike. Add your name at the end.

TÉLÉGRAMME

N° 698

Étiquettes

N° d'appel :

INDICATIONS DE TRANSMISSION

Ligne de numérotation

ZCZC

N° télégraphique

Taxe principale.

Timbre
à
date

Ligne pilote

Taxes
accessoires

N° de la ligne du P.V. :

Total . .

Bureau de destination   Département ou Pays

Bureau d'origine   Mots   Date   Heure   Mentions de service

Services spéciaux demandés :
(voir au verso)

Inscrire en **CAPITALES** l'adresse complète (rue, n° bloc, bâtiment, escalier, etc...), le texte et
la signature (une lettre par case ; **laisser une case blanche entre les mots**).

Nom et
adresse

TEXTE et éventuellement
signature très lisible

Pour accélérer la remise des télégrammes indiquer le cas échéant,
le numéro de téléphone (1) ou de télex du destinataire
TF _____ TLX _____

Pour avis en cas de non remise, indiquer le nom et l'adresse de l'expéditeur (2) :

728678 Y Imp. Mod. - Limoges

97 % des conducteurs de train appelés à la grève demain

S.N.C.F. : Graves perturbations sur la banlieue

51

11 Now that we are in the Common Market, it is easier to get a job in a country like France. You may like the idea of doing this after you leave school. Temporary jobs in France are one good way of improving your French. You might apply for an au pair job, or you might go abroad for a while as part of a college or university course, to work in an office, in a factory or to study.

If you apply to a French organization, you will have to fill in a form about yourself – a 'curriculum vitae' or CV. Here is an example of one. Copy it out, then fill in the details in legible handwriting.

```
                    CURRICULUM VITAE.


    NOM:
    PRENOM:
    NATIONALITE:
    ADRESSE:

    DATE DE NAISSANCE:
    SITUATION DE FAMILLE:

    ENSEIGNEMENT:

    DIPLOMES:

    EMPLOI:

    LOISIRS / PASSETEMPS:

    SPORTS PRACTIQUES:

    VOYAGES:

    DISPONIBLE A PARTIR DE:

    AUTRES DETAILS:



    DATE:                   SIGNE:
```

(You may also be asked to write a letter about yourself. Such a letter is featured in the letter-writing section on page 87–88. You may like to do these two exercises together.)

12 The French railway company (SNCF) offers a travel and holiday service to all parts of France and the continent. You can book in advance for a wide variety of excursions, from those lasting a single day to others of several days' duration.

Here are four such possibilities, taken from their brochure.

Châteaux de la Loire

Loches, Chenonceaux, Amboise

Départs samedis
15 juin
6 juillet
14 septembre

398 f

tout compris
sauf boissons
(entrées comprises)

Départ de Paris-Austerlitz vers 7 heures en places assises de 2ᵉ classe. Arrivée à Tours vers 9 h 20.
Départ en autocar pour Loches (visite du château).
Déjeuner. Continuation pour Chenonceaux (visite) et Amboise (visite). Retour à Tours. Départ vers 18 h 20. Arrivée à Paris-Austerlitz vers 20 h 30.
Dîner libre.

Les plages du débarquement

Départs samedis 22 juin 10 août 7 septembre

372 f

tout compris
sauf entrées
et boissons

Départ de Paris-Saint-Lazare vers 9 h en places assises de 2ᵉ classe. Arrivée à Caen vers 11 h 30. Déjeuner. Départ en autocar : Bayeux (mémorial anglais), Omaha Beach (mémorial et nécropole américains), Port-en-Bessin. Arromanches (musée du Débarquement), Courseulles, Lion-sur-Mer, Colleville (monument Montgomery), Riva-Bella, Caen. Dîner libre. Départ vers 20 h 30. Arrivée à Paris vers 22 h 45.

Week-end à Najac en Rouergue

Voyage individuel départs les vendredis du 3 mai au 27 septembre

820 f

tout compris
sauf boissons

Vendredi : Départ de Paris-Austerlitz vers 21 h 30 en places assises de 2ᵉ classe. (Possibilité de couchettes avec supplément).
Samedi : Arrivée à Najac vers 6 h 30. Transfert. Petit déjeuner. Déjeuner. Dîner. Logement. (Possibilité de profiter des installations de la résidence et de la piscine, promenades à pied, excursions).
Dimanche : Petit déjeuner. Déjeuner. Dîner. Transfert à la gare. Départ vers 22 h 30 en places assises de 2ᵉ classe.
Lundi : Arrivée à Paris-Austerlitz vers 7 h 30.

Les inscriptions sont prises exclusivement le lundi pour départ le vendredi de la même semaine.

8 Le charme de la Camargue

Voyage AR par TGV

Départs
5 avril
(Pâques)
24 mai
(Pentecôte)
13 septembre

1 690 f
tout compris
sauf boissons
et entrées

1er jour : Départ de Paris gare de Lyon par TGV en places assises de 2e classe vers 10 h. Déjeuner libre. Arrivée en Avignon vers 14 h. Départ en autocar. Visite d'Arles. Dîner et logement.

2e jour : Petit déjeuner. Départ pour une excursion de la journée en Camargue : tour rapide dans la Camargue sauvage, arrivée au domaine de la Belugrie, visite de la manade sur des chariots tractés. Retour au mas : apéritif et repas dans la bergerie.
Jeux de Gardians, vachettes emboulées pour les amateurs. Retour à l'hôtel en longeant l'étang de Vaccarès. Arrêt pour dégustation au Mas de Rey.
Dîner et logement.

3e jour : Petit déjeuner. Matinée libre. Départ Déjeuner. Transfert à la gare d'Avignon. Départ par TGV vers 15 h. Arrivée à Paris gare de Lyon vers 19 h.

While on holiday in Paris you decide to take one of these excursions. (The one-day visits are numbers 1 and 2; the longer ones are 8 and 14.)

You will need to fill in the form from the back of the brochure (see over) in French, with your details.

You are with your mother, father and brother (he is under 12 years old). If you require a single room for anyone, there is a supplement of 50 francs per night. Your father will pay by cheque. Your address in France is the Hotel Molière, Rue Molière, Paris 10. Tel: 294657. (Make up an appropriate date.)

a) Choose a one-day excursion and complete the application form (in French).
b) Next, choose a longer excursion and complete the application form (in French).

BULLETIN D'INSCRIPTION

à compléter et à adresser à
TOURISME SNCF
VENTE PAR CORRESPONDANCE
B.P. 62
75362 PARIS CEDEX 08

Important : le montant doit être joint à ce bulletin. Mode de réglement établi à l'ordre des BUREAUX DE TOURISME DE LA SNCF (1)

☐ virement postal   ☐ chèque bancaire   ☐ mandat-lettre

Je soussigné (e), (2) ....

adresse et téléphone : ....

accompagné (e) de .... personnes (3)
(indiquer l'âge pour les enfants de moins de 12 ans).

            • .... • ....
(2)
            • .... • ....

demande à être inscrit (e) pour le voyage ou séjour suivant :

Date de départ .... durée ....jours

portant le n° .... de cette brochure.

Prix forfaitaire F : .... × .... [   ]

chambre individuelle F : .... × .... [   ]

supplément voyage 1ʳᵉ classe F : .... × .... [   ]

supplément voyage voiture-lit F : .... × .... [   ]

Total F : [   ]

Chambres (1)

Grand lit (2 personnes)   ☐

Deux lits (2 personnes)   ☐

Individuelle (1 personne)   ☐

J'ai pris connaissance des conditions générales et des conditions particulières.

(date et signature)

(1) Mettre une croix dans la case correspondante.
(2) Nom et prénoms en capitales.
(3) Nombre de personnes.

56

13 While in France you notice that there is a cheap adverts section in the local paper. You are staying· for three weeks in a *gîte* in Alsace. You decide to ask for young French people to play tennis or go swimming with you and to talk to you in French to help you improve.

You are staying in a village called Ostheim and the address is 2, Route de Riquewhir. Explain what you need in the advert but write between twenty-five and thirty words only.

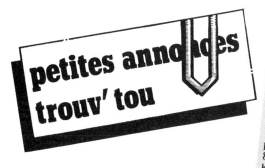

de François, choix important. Prix à débattre. Réponse assurée.

Silvia GAILLARD (Paris). Avis aux amateurs de théâtre ! J'ai 14 ans et aimerais former une troupe de garçons et filles passionnés de théâtre (surtout classique) de 13 à 16 ans, pendant l'année scolaire 80/81 à Paris. Att. nombreuses rép.

Valérie STEPHAN (Finistère). Rech. posters, affiches sur la belle époque, représentant des costumes. Esp. nombreuses réponses.

Roselyne GUERIN (Orne). Vds livres classes 4e, 3e¦ Liste sur demande. Prixà débattre. C'est urgent.

Isabelle   GASQUEZ (Loire). Remercie déjà celles qui me donneront des documents et photos sur la danse classique. Encore merci.

14 Unfortunately, while in the same *gîte*, you discover that your bicycle has been stolen. You report it to the police, but decide to put an advert in the local paper, *Les Dernières Nouvelles d'Alsace*, in the hope of getting it back.

Say it was stolen at Hunewhir, near the zoo, on Tuesday 11th August. It is a British bike, red, and has your name on it. Give your French address and offer 100 francs as a reward.

Particuliers ██ Services 🐿️

parait tous les mardis

Bon d'insertion (réservé exclusivement aux particuliers)

à remettre ou à adresser avec votre paiement à l'agence des **Dernières Nouvelles**
la plus proche (en précisant «Particuliers DN Services» **d'Alsace**
sur votre enveloppe).

Nom _____ Prénom _____

Adresse _____

TEXTE DE L'ANNONCE EN LETTRES MAJUSCULES : (une lettre ou signe par case, laisser une case libre entre chaque mot)

▶ Les 4 lignes
70 F

▶ La ligne
en plus
+ 16 F

Les ordres devront nous
parvenir au plus tard le
vendredi précédant
la parution, avant 10 h
TOTAL A PAYER .... Signature :

Rubrique : ....
par CCP ☐
chèque bancaire ☐
espèces (guichet) ☐

Attention ! Particuliers DN Services n'accepte ni offres d'emploi, ni ventes et achats immeubles, appartements, ni annonces sous chiffre.

---

15 While in France, you see some things you like in a mail-order catalogue and decide to place an order. The catalogue order form is shown on the next page.

Write out, in French, details for the following order:
a) Dress – red; Size 38; Quantity – 1; Price – 130 francs; Code X 439 A
b) Shoes – blue; Size 38; Quantity – 1; Price – 200 francs; Code Y 269 L
c) Wallet – brown; Quantity – 1; Price – 80 francs; Code W 462 B

The total cost will be 410 francs, so there is no postage to pay. Don't forget to fill in your French address: 7, Avenue Becquart, Lambersart 59130.

Unit 5 WRITING LETTERS

Writing letters is one of the most useful skills you will learn in the course of your French lessons. It is one of the most common forms of writing you will need in the world beyond school. A well-written letter can help form good friends and, in the world of business, a well-written letter can be most impressive.

Letter-writing is certainly a skill that will be tested in your GCSE examination, so here are some useful tips to help you with the practice which follows.

There are three types of letters which you may be asked to write. These are:

a) **'Official' letters**, for example to hotels, camp-sites, companies and official organizations such as Tourist Offices.

b) **Informal letters to friends** and acquaintances of your own age.

c) **Formal letters to adults** as individuals – such as thank you letters.

Hints on writing letters

Whatever type of letter you are asked to write, there are always distinct sections to include and it is always very important to keep in mind the person to whom you are writing.

The sections are as follows:
a) **The opening greeting**: 'Dear . . . '
b) **The introduction** – the pleasant phrases: 'thank you', etc.
c) **The main point of the letter** – the main message.
d) **The conclusion**: 'Hope to see you soon', etc.
e) **Signing off**: 'Yours sincerely', etc.

Starting and finishing the letter
It is important to match the formula to the type of letter that you are writing.

	STARTING	FINISHING
1	Official letters	
	Monsieur	*Veuillez agréer, Monsieur*
	Madame	*(Madame), l'expression de*
		mes sentiments distingués.
2	Informal letters to friends	
	Cher Paul	*Amicalement*
	Chère Annie	*Amitiés*
	Salut!	*Bons baisers*
	Cher ami	*Grosses bises*
	Chère amie	*Ton ami(e)*
		A bientôt
		Affectueusement
3	Formal letters to adults	
	Cher Monsieur	*Avec mes remerciements*
	Chère Madame	*Bien cordialement*
	Chers Madame et	
	Monsieur	*Salutations distingués*

Don't forget to use the *tu* form (and *ton, ta, tes*) when writing to friends. Use the more formal *vous* (and *votre, vos*), when writing any other sort of letter.

61

Useful expressions

When writing letters, we have in mind several functions or purposes. We may be asking for something, saying thank you, making excuses, accepting or declining an invitation, complaining or simply gossiping!

Here are some useful expressions which will help you do these things:

INFORMAL LETTERS	OFFICIAL/FORMAL LETTERS
Thanking	
Je te remercie de ta dernière lettre.	*Je vous remercie de votre lettre.*
Je te remercie de la carte postale.	*J'accuse réception de votre lettre du 10 octobre.*
Ta dernière lettre m'a fait beaucoup de plaisir.	*Je vous remercie de vos brochures.*
Merci beaucoup pour le cadeau.	
Asking for help/information	
Peux-tu me dire . . .	*Je voudrais savoir*
Veux-tu m'envoyer . . .	*Pourriez-vous m'envoyer*
Je voudrais savoir . . .	*Je vous serais reconnaissant(e) de me faire savoir . . .*
	Veuillez m'envoyer . . .
	Je serais très reconnaissant(e) si vous pouviez . . .
Making excuses	
Pardonne-moi de ne pas avoir écrit (téléphoné) . . .	*J'ai le regret de vous faire savoir que . . .*
J'espère que tu me pardonneras . . .	*Veuillez accepter mes excuses les plus sincères . . .*
Je suis désolé(e) d'avoir	

62

te dire que . . .

Accepting/declining
*Je suis très heureux
(heureuse) d'accepter . . .
Je regrette, mais . . .*

Making comments/judgements
*C'est très bien; C'est fantastique; Je suis furieux
(furieuse); Je suis étonné(e)/surpris(e); J'espère
que; Je suis content(e) que; Je suis désolé(e); Je
suis déçu(e); Je préfère; J'aimerais; Félicitations;
C'est bien triste.*

Writing addresses
When writing a letter to France, it is normal to
write the address of the sender on the back of the
envelope.

Don't forget to make a note of the sender's address
on any letter you may receive from France, before
you throw away the envelope, as the full address
may not be written on the top of the letter itself.

Final checkpoints

1 Decide who it is you are writing to – is it a *tu* or
   vous letter?
2 If you have a letter to answer, read through
   the original carefully and note all the things
   you are asked to do – the information required
   and the questions to be answered.
3 Only copy and use the words of the original
   letter when necessary.
4 In a friendly letter it is a good idea to ask a
   question or two yourself – expecting a reply.
5 Make sure that you have an appropriate
   ending.

1 Here is a letter written by a young French person. Read it through carefully and notice how it is set out. Make a note of the questions that are asked as well as the information given.

When you have read it, write your reply. Make sure that you answer all the questions. Imagine that it is a letter to your penfriend, to whom you write fairly often. Write about 100 words in French.

> 25 rue Eugène Varlin
> 75010 Paris
>
> Paris le 17 Mars 86
>
> Cher Peter,
>
> Merci bien pour ta gentille lettre qui vient d'arriver. Ce week-end, je me suis bien amusé: samedi après-midi j'ai fait une partie de tennis avec des amis et le soir, nous sommes allés aux Champs Elysées voir un film de science-fiction, c'était formidable! Puis, le dimanche, comme il faisait un temps superbe, on est tous allés faire une promenade au bois de Boulogne.
>
> Je te remercie de m'avoir invité au mariage de ton cousin Thierry. Je lui ai acheté un beau service de verres en cristal, j'espère que ça lui plaira. Bientôt ce sera les vacances, moi je pars dans les Alpes et toi? Pourras-tu venir nous voir cet été? Je serai de retour à Paris le 1er août. Si tu viens, quand penses-tu arriver et où?
>
> Dis-moi un peu ce que tu aimerais bien faire quand tu seras chez nous.
>
> Ecris-moi vite et surtout donne bien le bonjour à tes parents de ma part.   Jean-Michel.

Here are some more letters for you to write. These are shorter and are for a specific purpose.

It is sometimes necessary to write a polite letter to say thank you or to accept, for example, an invitation. Imagine that you have had the following letters from your French friends. Write a suitable reply to each one of them, in French.

2 You have just received the following letter from a penfriend accepting your invitation to spend two weeks with you in Britain.

22 rue de la Parcheminerie
75005 Paris

Paris le 5 avril 86

Chère Beverley,
Je te remercie beaucoup de ta lettre qui m'a fait très plaisir. Bien entendu, je suis tout à fait enchantée d'accepter ton invitation à venir passer deux semaines à Leeds, c'est une excellente idée !
Demain, j'irai réserver une place pour le train qui part de la gare du Nord à 8H30 le matin, j'arriverai donc à Leeds vers 19H30, j'espère que tu voudras m'attendre.
Aimerais-tu que j'achète quelque chose, dis-moi ce qui plairait à tes parents, peut-être un petit souvenir de Paris.
Est-ce que tu voudrais revenir en France avec moi, mes parents seraient contents si tu pouvais aussi passer une quinzaine de jours avec nous à Annecy.
Écris-moi vite pour me dire ce que tu en penses. J'espère que tu pourras.
Bien amicalement.
Marie-Claire

65

You have been invited this year to spend two weeks with your penfriend's family at Annecy in the Alps. Write a polite reply, in French, accepting the offer.

Say that you will travel by air and hope to leave on 3rd August. You will fly from London to Lyon and will arrive at 13.00 h.. You are looking forward to the holiday. You like walking and playing tennis, so you will bring a racket. Say you will write later to ask if there is anything she would like you to bring from England.

3   You have now had an invitation to spend Christmas in France with your penfriend. Write back accepting (in French).

Say you can't leave before 20th December – the end of your school term. Ask what the weather is like in France in December. Ask too what presents you should bring for the rest of the family.

Say there will be a surprise for your friend. You will telephone soon with travel plans. Ask one or two questions about what you will do over the Christmas holidays.

Sometimes you have to refuse an invitation for one reason or another. But you must do it politely so as not to offend. Here is an example of such a letter.

Rimiez Supérieur
Cité des Castors
06 Nice

Nice, le 18 février 86

Cher Christopher,

Je te remercie de ta lettre que je viens de recevoir et je m'empresse d'y répondre. C'était très gentil de m'inviter à venir passer quelques jours chez toi; malheureusement je ne peux pas accepter car ma mère est très malade, elle doit rester au lit et je dois l'aider; mon père travaille toute la journée et il ne pourrait pas se débrouiller tout seul pour faire la cuisine, le ménage et les courses.

Mais si tout va bien, je serais content de te revoir à Pâques car j'ai deux semaines de vacances.

Inutile de te dire combien je suis déçu, pardonne-moi, j'aurais tellement aimé venir te voir.

A bientôt j'espère.

Amitiés

Laurent

Now here are some examples for you to try.

4 Your Swiss (French-speaking) friend has invited you to Switzerland for the Whitsuntide holidays.

Write a polite refusal (in French), saying that your parents have already booked a holiday in Scotland and that you are going with them. Suggest another time for your visit to Switzerland.

5 You have just had this invitation to a party while you are in France.

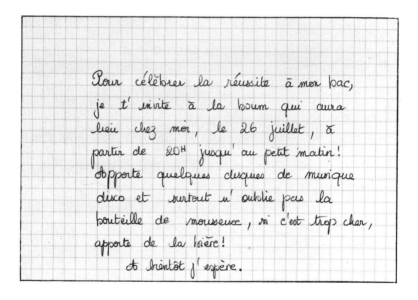

Pour célébrer la réussite à mon bac, je t'invite à la boum qui aura lieu chez moi, le 26 juillet, à partir de 20H jusqu'au petit matin! Apporte quelques disques de musique disco et surtout n'oublie pas la bouteille de mousseux, si c'est trop cher, apporte de la bière!
À bientôt j'espère.

You are going to the theatre that evening, so are unable to go.

Write a polite refusal and say that you hope the party will be good.

6 While in France you receive an invitation to go to the cinema with a boy (or girl) you met on the beach. You are not keen to go out with him/her and so you write a polite letter to say no.

You must find a reasonable excuse so as not to offend. (Think of your own excuses this time – but be reasonable!) Write your letter in French.

Writing letters of thanks is always a nice thing to do. Look at this example.

Mᵉˡˡᵉ Sylvie Reynaud
21, Rue de la République
38 000 Grenoble

Grenoble le 2.1.86

Chère Debbie,

Merci beaucoup pour ta carte et aussi pour le cadeau d'anniversaire que tu m'as envoyé J'ai beaucoup aimé le livre sur Leeds. Merci encore.

Pour mon anniversaire, j'ai invité 5 de mes amis, nous avons écouté de la musique et nous avons mangé tous ensemble.

Au fait quel est le jour de ton anniversaire ? As-tu l'intention de faire une boum, que vas-tu préparer à dîner pour tes amis ? Dis-moi aussi quel cadeau te ferait plaisir ? A bientôt. Grosses bises
Sylvie

Now, here are two examples for you to try.

7   Write a letter in French to your friend just after your birthday. Thank him/her for the card and the record. Say you liked the record very much and that you had an enjoyable party with your friends.

8   While in France, you spend a weekend in the *gîte* belonging to your friend's family.

Afterwards, write a letter of thanks, in French, to say that you enjoyed the weekend. You enjoyed the walks and also the meals. Mention something special that you ate, and that you did during the weekend.

Established in 1955 to promote rural tourism

Federation Nationale des Gîtes Ruraux de France

9, avenue Georges V
75008 PARIS
Tel: 723.77.30

Gîtes de France Ltd.
178 Piccadilly
LONDON W1V 0AL

You have just had a letter from your French penfriend who is coming to stay with you for a while during the summer holidays. Although you have written to each other for some time, you have never met. This is the letter you receive.

106 Avenue Philippe Auguste
75012 Paris

Paris le 16 Juin 86

Chère Lindsey,

Merci de m'avoir invité à passer une semaine à Londres, je suis tout à fait enchantée.

Je prendrai l'avion à Roissy et j'arriverai à l'aéroport de Heathrow samedi prochain à 14ʰ30.

Tu n'auras aucune difficulté à me reconnaître; voici une brève description : je suis assez grande et mince, j'ai les cheveux blonds et très longs.

Ce jour là, je porterai une jupe plissée rouge et un chemisier bleu marine - S'il fait froid, j'aurai aussi une veste blanche, un sac à main blanc et une énorme valise noire!

Dis-moi, que ferons-nous quand je serai chez toi? Si on allait visiter le Palais de Buckingham et la Tour de Londres - Ça serait chouette!

A samedi, grosses bises.

Karine

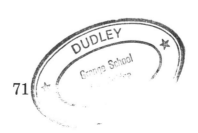

71

9 Now you are going to France for the first time and so you write to your penfriend to explain your plans. You haven't travelled alone before.

Thank your friend and her family for the invitation. Say that you will leave London by train at 9.45 a.m. on (make up the date) and will cross by boat to Boulogne. From there, you will take a train to Paris, arriving at the Gare du Nord at 17.50 h.

Say what you look like and what you will be wearing. You will have a rucksack. You hope to meet at the luggage office.

Ask what you will be doing during your stay, as well as anything else you wish to know.

10 Writing to a penfriend is a good way of improving your French and getting to know France. On the opposite page are some adverts for penfriends.

Here is an explanation of some of the abbreviations commonly used by the young people in these advertisements:
Souh. cor. avec F. ou G. = Souhaite correspondre avec fille ou garçon
rép ass = Réponse assurée
Aim. cor. av. = Aimerait correspondre avec

Choose the advertisement that interests you most and write the first letter to introduce yourself. Speak of your family, your house and your interests. Invite him/her to write back. Write your letter in French.

qui veut correspondre avec moi?

nous les filles

nous les garçons

Nicole JENDREJESKI (Morbihan). Souh. cor. av. F. ou G. 14/16 ans, tous pays, sachant parler français, anglais, ou allemand. Attirée par : la danse, le disco, le rock, les voyages, le sport, le cinéma. Joindre photo si poss.

Marie-Christine BASTIN (Loire). Souh. cor. av. F. ou G. 13/15 ans, parlant français. Attirée par : les animaux, la nature, le cinéma, le rire, la mode. Esp. recevoir nomb. lettres. Joindre photo si poss. Rép. assu.

Lydie STERBECQ (Nord). Echange cartes postales du Nord contre celles de tous pays. Rép. ass. Merci.

Albert ARNAULT (Loiret). Souh. cor. av. F. 14/16 ans, hab. la France. Aime : le hard-rock, le cinéma, les vacances. Joindre photo si possible.

Laurence MORILLOT (Aube). Ech. timbres de ts pays, oblitérés ou non.

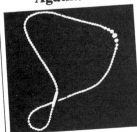

73

11 In a second letter to your penfriend, write about your school. Describe a typical day and send a copy of your timetable, in French. Ask about school in France – the starting times, clubs and activities, where they eat lunch, etc. You might like to add some questions of your own. Write your letter in French.

12 During the school holidays, you forget to write to your penfriend. You then receive a letter asking why you haven't written and what you did during the summer.

Write back to apologize and say why you didn't write – you had a job in the supermarket for four weeks to earn money and then you went camping with some friends in the Lake District.

Write a few details about your time there and what you did. Say that you hope to hear from your friend soon. Write your letter in French.

13 While in France, you and your friend booked a five-day cycling holiday in the area of the Lot, as suggested by the advertisement opposite. Write a letter home to describe what you did during the five days, where you stayed, what you saw, what the meals were like, and the people you met (mention a picnic, nice scenery, swimming in a lake, for example).

Write about 120 words (in French), plus the usual greetings and endings.

Vacances actives

Randonnées à bicyclette

LOCATION DE VÉLOS

Aux amoureux de la nature nous proposons des randonnées à bicyclette sur les petites routes pittoresques et peu fréquentées de la campagne lotoise. Puy-L'Évêque sera votre point de départ et vous visiterez successivement Bonaguil, Villefranche du Périgord, Cazals, Cénac, Domme, Catus, Luzech et Albas.

Caractéristiques

— Randonnée à bicyclette de 5 jours
— Début du séjour à Puy-L'Évêque (possibilité d'être hébergé sous tente la veille au soir et le dernier soir)
— Pension complète (hébergement en gîtes d'étape ou petits hôtels ; repas froids à midi).
— Prêts de vélos cyclotouristes 10 vitesses avec sacoches
Validité : du 1er juin au 15 octobre

Prix : Réf. V 1A

950 F par personne
La journée supplémentaire : 180 F.

LOCATION A L'HEURE

A LA DEMI-JOURNÉE

A LA JOURNÉE

A LA SEMAINE

14 You wish to exchange houses with a family in France during the summer holidays and have been sent this cutting from a French paper. The house sounds ideal and so your parents (who don't speak French) ask you to write a letter in French for them.

> Stella-Plage (près Du Touquet, 62.) Boulevard de la Mer. 200 m de la plage, à 300 m des commerces. Près de la piscine. Villa indépendante, cuisine, salon (TV), cuisine équipée, 3 chambres (1 lit à une personne, 2 lits à 2 pers., salle de bains, chauffage central, garage, pelouse jardin pour enfants. A proximité: tennis, ski nautique. Exchange vacances juillet/août. Tel: 30.42.49

In your letter, ask if you can exchange houses for one month (August). To help the French family you should, in addition to stating the dates, write a brief description of your own house and its facilities.

In order to tempt the French family to come over, mention one or two things they could do in the area during their stay.

15 Write a letter, in French, to your penfriend to tell him/her about your holiday job.

You have been working to save to buy something. Say what you did, what time you started each day, what exactly you did while at work (perhaps there was an amusing incident).

Say if you liked the job or not and also say how you will spend the money. Ask if he/she worked during the holidays.

16 While in France on holiday, you meet a boy or girl on the beach and you spend the day together. You get on well. Unfortunately, you don't know where he/she lives but would like to meet again so . . .

Write, in French, to a teenage magazine. Say where you met, and when. Describe what you were wearing and what you did that day. Give your telephone number and ask him/her to contact you . . . !

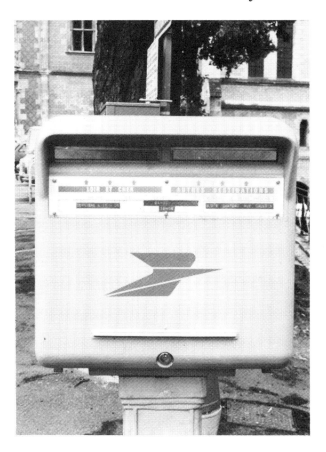

Unit 6 *WRITING FORMAL LETTERS*

If you are planning to visit France for your holidays, you will want to get as much information as possible about the area where you intend to stay. A good way of doing this is to write to the local Tourist Office. In France these are called *Office de Tourisme* or *Syndicat d'Initiative*. They offer all kinds of services for visitors. They will supply maps of the area, visitors' guides, lists of hotels, restaurants and campsites, for example, and much more besides.

To make sure that you get a reply, include an international reply coupon (*un coupon-réponse-international*) which you can get from your local post office.

79

Here is a typical letter to a Tourist Office:

100, Basford Road,
Nottingham NG6 0JG
le 5 février 87.

Le Directeur,
L'Office de Tourisme
Colmar 68000
France.

Monsieur,

J'ai l'intention de visiter l'Alsace au mois de juillet. Veuillez m'envoyer des brochures sur votre région ainsi qu'une liste des monuments touristiques. Je m'intéresse au vin d'Alsace et je voudrais visiter des caves.

Veuillez agréer, Monsieur, l'expression de mes sentiments distingués

R Searby

1 Imagine that you have decided to go to the Loire Valley for your holidays. Write a letter, in French, to the Tourist Office in Tours asking for information about the town and the region. In particular you would like a list of hotels and restaurants, details of excursions in the area and a map of the town.

TOURS

BUREAU DE LA CHAÎNE NATIONALE
D'ACCUEIL ET D'INFORMATION

ACCUEIL DE FRANCE

PLACE M^{AL}-LECLERC
37042 TOURS Cedex

Tél. 47.05.58.08   Télex 750008

Office de Tourisme

2 Now write to the Tourist Office in Blois. You would like a list of campsites in the area, details of the *châteaux* that you can visit, and information about the sports facilities available. Write your letter in French.

A TRAVERS BLOIS : un peu d'Histoire SIGHTSEEING IN BLOIS : places of interest SEHENSWÜRDIGKEITEN

A. CHATEAU – MUSEE ROBERT HOUDIN
Du château-fort des comtes de Blois au château de Gaston d'Orléans en passant par celui de Charles d'Orléans et les demeures royales de Louis XII et François 1er, cinq siècles d'Histoire s'inscrivent dans la pierre.
Une salle consacrée à Robert HOUDIN a été installée au château de Blois. On y a souligné les différentes facettes du génie de cet illustre Blésois. Les vitrines évoquent non seulement le prestidigitateur qui fit courir toute l'Europe, mais aussi l'horloger, l'homme de science passionné d'électricité, de physique, d'ophtalmologie et l'écrivain.
A. THE CHATEAU – ROBERT HOUDIN MUSEUM
From the fortified castle of the Counts of Blois to the palatial wing of Gaston d'Orléans, through the court of Charles d'Orléans and the royal dwellings of Louis XII and Francis I, five centuries of history are embodied in the stone.
One room dedicated to Robert HOUDIN has been opened in the Chateau of Blois

81

3 Write to the Tourist Office in Langeais to say that you wish to spend a few days there. Ask for a list of hotels, and for information on what there is to see and do.

If you have any special interests yourself (for example, sport or history) ask about them too.

Write your letter in French.

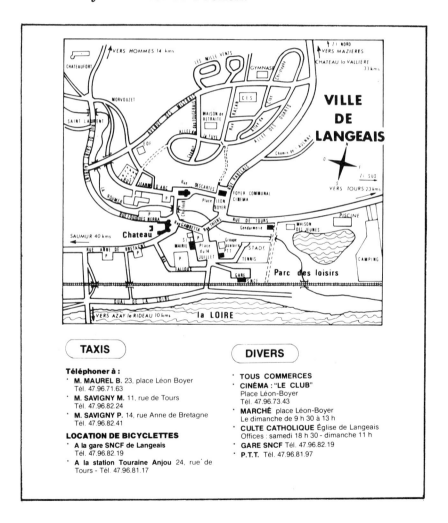

Having decided on the place for your holiday, you should now write to a hotel, campsite or Youth Hostel in order to arrange your stay.

The *Hôtel de la Renaissance* in Blois is the one you have chosen. Here is the letter that you have received from the manager.

HÔTEL RENAISSANCE

9, rue du Pont du Gast

Tél. 54.78.02.63

41000 BLOIS

R.C. BLOIS A 325 429 736

Blois   le 19 juillet 1986

à

Monsieur Morris,
Leeds, Grande Bretagne.

Monsieur,
      J'ai bien reçu votre lettre du 12 courant me demandant de réserver une chambre pour 2 personnes avec douche et WC privés et une chambre à deux lits pour les enfants, du samedi 23 / 8 / 86 au mercredi 27 / 8 / 86 non compris.
      Je peux satisfaire votre demande à la condition que vous m'envoyiez un Eurochèque de 200 F Français pour confirmer votre réservation.
      Le prix de la chambre pour deux personnes avec douche WC privés est de 135 F et le prix de la chambre à deux lits est de 170 F; le petit déjeuner coûte 18,50.
      Dans l'attente d'avoir le plaisir de vous voir,
Veuillez croire, Monsieur, à l'expression de mes sentiments dévoués,

J.Crespin.

4 What letter did you write in the first place to the hotel?

Write it in French as if you had written on behalf of your parents, yourself and your brother (or sister).

5 On another occasion, the *Hôtel de la Renaissance* is unable to give you accommodation. Here is the letter you have received from the manager. Read it, then write to the *Hôtel de la Croix Blanche* to confirm the arrangements.

HOTEL RENAISSANCE

9, rue du Pont du Gast

41000 BLOIS   Tél. 54.78.02.63

R.C. BLOIS A 325 429 736

Blois, le 20 Août 86.

à

Monsieur Morris,

Leeds.

Monsieur,

J'ai bien reçu votre lettre du 15 août me demandant de vous réserver deux chambres pour le 14 et 15 septembre 1986. Je n'ai malheureusement plus de chambres disponibles pour cette période mais l'Hôtel de la Croix Blanche, à Blois, avec lequel j'ai pris contact peut vous recevoir dans les mêmes conditions.

Veuillez prendre dès que possible vos dispositions avec cet hôtel dont vous trouverez l'adresse ci-jointe. Il serait bon de joindre un Eurochèque de 200FF pour confirmer votre réservation.

Dans l'espoir de pouvoir vous recevoir un jour dans notre hôtel, croyez, Monsieur Morris, à l'expression de nos sentiments dévoués,

J.Crespin.

84

6 On your way through France you decide to spend one night at Alençon, a small town north of Le Mans. A friend recommends the *Hôtel de France.*

Write, in French, to the manager. Ask if there is a room free for the night of June 17th. Say there are two of you and you want a twin room with shower. Ask the price of the room. Ask if there is a garage at the hotel. Ask if the hotel is near the town centre.

7 One year you are hoping to go camping in France and like the look of the site on the Ile d'Or – the island in the middle of the River Loire at Amboise.

Write, in French, to the campsite manager (we will call him Jean-Pierre Menet). Say you wish to spend two weeks there, from Saturday 14th August to Saturday 28th August. Ask if there are any pitches free. Say how many tents you have and how many people there will be. Ask for the prices and a leaflet about the site.

8 You decide one year to hire a *gîte* in France for your holidays. You have found the address in the Guide to *gîtes* and so you write, in French, to the owner to ask if there are any vacancies for the first two weeks in August.

State the number of people in your family or group and ask the cost per week. Ask what facilities the *gîte* offers, the number of rooms, etc. Include an international reply coupon.

(E 6)	**JUNG Roger** - 23, rue de la 1ʳᵉ Armée　　　　　　　Tél. 89.47.92.17
N° 1	1 chambre à 2 lits pour 1 pers., cuisine avec 1 lit pour 1 pers., frigo, W.C. + douche privés, chauf. central, parking privé, confort, prix 900 F la semaine
N° 3	1 chambre à 1 lit pour 2 pers., coin cuisine, frigo, lavabo, W.C. + douche privés, chauf. central, parking privé, confortable. Prix 785 F la semaine
N' 4	Appartement 4 pers., 1 chambre avec 1 lit 2 pers., 1 chambre avec 2 lits superposés 1 pers., salle de séjour, cuisine, s.d.b., WC privés, chauff. électr., cour, parking, prix 1200 F la semaine
N° 5	Studio 2 à 3 pers. : 1 chambre avec 1 lit 2 pers., salle de séjour avec banquette-lit, coin cuisine, salle d'eau, douche, lavabo, WC privés, chauff. élect., cour, parking, prix 950 F la semaine
(H 3)	**MEYER Arno** - 7, rue du 5 décembre　　　　　　　Tél. 89.47.92.12 Chambres avec cuisine.

9 Imagine that, on returning home, you discover that you have lost your camera. You think you may have left it in your hotel.

Write a letter, in French, to the manager, explaining that you have lost the camera. Mention the date of your stay, the number of your room while there and say that the camera was marked with your name.

As you are not going back to France this year, say that your French friend (make up a name and address) will collect it on your behalf.

10 Write a letter, in French, to the *Bureau des Objets Trouvés* in Boulogne, where you spent a short time, to say that you lost a briefcase in the town.

State several objects that your briefcase contained and ask if it has been found. Mention the dates that you were in the town, and several possible places that you visited, where you might have lost it.

Give your address for the return and say that you will pay the postage costs.

11 It is becoming easier to work abroad. If you are a student, you may have to work abroad for a short while as part of your course. After you leave school you may wish to work as an au pair to improve your French. If so, you may have to write a letter to apply for such a post.

You have just seen these adverts in a paper. Write, in French, to one family concerned, giving your personal details – age, education, experience, etc. Don't forget to state why you think you will be suitable for the post and when you will be free.

You may ask for some details as well, such as the ages of the children, working hours, etc.

You may not like the idea of looking after children! There are other possibilities, especially if you can speak French. It is sometimes possible to work in a *Colonie de vacances* as a group leader, in a campsite as a sports organizer, at harvest-time as an auxiliary worker or even in the hotel business, especially in areas where there are a lot of British visitors.

In England, the Central Bureau for Educational Visits and Exchanges, Seymour Mews House, Seymour Mews, Wigmore St, London, W1H 9PE might help. They publish brochures with ideas.

Here are two ideas.

12 Look at the advertisement below. Write to the campsite (via the HAVAS agency in Béziers) to apply for the post as sports leader for the holiday period.

Say why you are interested, what qualifications you have for the job, any experience you have, etc. Say that you are including a curriculum vitae (see page 52).

You may wish to ask some questions yourself. Write your letter in French.

13 The advertisement below is for a job in a restaurant in the French-speaking part of Switzerland. Write a letter of application (in French).

Enclose full details of yourself and your experience. Sound enthusiastic about the possibility of working there. Don't forget to ask questions yourself on anything you wish to know.

service de jour, nourrie, logée
Tél. 19 41 27/55 33 26
36 RESTAURANT DE MONTAGNE
cherche   (497319
ETUDIANTES
18-20 ans environ, pour juillet-août
et septembre
CLEMENT SALAMIN
71 3961 Grimentz/Valais/Suisse
13 *Tél. 19 41 27/65 10 81*
Rest. «Les Halles du Pont»   (497315
14, rue des Moulins
67000 Strasbourg

HOTEL - BAR - RESTAURANT
tout confort

auberge
des Skieurs

RUE MONTLOSIER   *tél.* ✆ 259
LE MONT-DORE

89

14 You have at last secured that summer job! You will be travelling to France by train. You have written to the SNCF in Angers where you will be working, asking for timetables, fares, and the cost of travel from Paris. Below is the letter that you had from the information office.

RÉGION DE NANTES
CIRCONSCRIPTION
EXPLOITATION
D'ANGERS
Rue Denis Papin
49044 Angers Cedex
Tél. 41 88 78 01

Nos réf.
18/BC

Angers, le
25 Septembre 1986

Madame C.J. MORRIS
Caedmon Hall
Beckett Park
LEEDS
L S 6 3 QS
GRANDE-BRETAGNE

Madame,

Suite à votre lettre,j'ai l'honneur de vous transmettre ci-jointe une fiche horaire valable à partir du 28 Septembre et de vous communiquer ci-après les prix aller et retour - ANGERS - PARIS au plein tarif.

        1ère classe   : 412 Francs
        2ème classe   : 274 Francs

Restant à votre disposition pour toutes informations complémentaires, je vous prie d'agréer, Madame, l'expression de mes respectueux hommages.

LE CHEF DE BUREAU VOYAGEURS,

Ch. BURTIN.

Société Nationale des
Chemins de fer Français
R.C.S. Paris B 552 049 447

Write out your original letter to SNCF (in French). Mention all the details you require, not forgetting the date of your proposed journey (that is important since the price can vary according to the time of travel). Ask for a reply as soon as possible.

Unit 7 *WRITING STORIES AND ESSAYS*

Writing stories is not always easy, so make sure that you read these helpful hints beforehand.

1   Find out before you start exactly how many words you should write.

2   Keep your French simple and as accurate as possible.

3   If you are not sure about something, don't use it. Employ some other French phrase.

4   Read through the instructions or outline very carefully, before writing anything at all.

5   Make sure that you know what tense you are to use.

6   Plan an outline so as to include all the parts of the story.

7   Decide if you are to be in the story (sometimes you will be told to do this). If that is the case, remember it will involve the use of *je* and *nous*.

8   Use a variety of French expressions. Some things you will have learnt off by heart will be useful here – but only use such items when they are appropriate to the story.

9   Use what you know and avoid at all costs thinking out the story in English and then translating it.

10   Link each section or episode with link words or phrases such as *puis, une heure plus tard, immédiatement, sans* + infinitive, etc.

11 Try to use some complex sentences with two sections linked by *qui, parce que,* etc.

12 Avoid using English words to fill the gaps. Avoid also too many English words such as names of pop groups – this won't gain you marks.

Finally – **revise what you write**. Remember the slogan: 'careless errors cost marks'. Check verb endings, genders, agreements, etc.

A Writing stories from an outline

1 Your school is linked with the Lycée Jean Perrin in France and your class has been exchanging letters and projects with a similar class there on a regular basis.

You have been asked to write an account of a class outing made last week. Write about 130 words, in French, saying where you went, how you travelled, what you did and if you enjoyed the outing.

2 You have been on a school outing to France and stayed for three days in Dieppe. Using the material from the map and the guide book, write, in French, a short account (130 words) of the stay, stating what you did, where you stayed, the activities and walks you enjoyed.

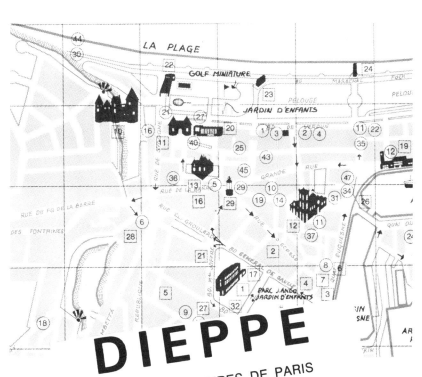

DIEPPE

LA MER À 2 HEURES DE PARIS

PLAGE

1 800 MÈTRES DE RIVAGE, 8 HECTARES DE PELOUSES, TRÈS VASTES PARKINGS GRATUITS DE 610 PLACES ■ PISCINE OLYMPIQUE D'EAU DE MER CHAUFFÉE (24°) OUVERTE DU 1ᵉʳ MAI AU 30 SEPTEMBRE : 5 F ET 4 F ■ GOLF MINIATURE OUVERT DU 22 MARS AU 18 OCTOBRE : 3 F ■ JARDIN D'ENFANTS GRATUIT OUVERT DU 21 MARS AU 1ᵉʳ OCTOBRE (NOMBREUX JEUX, PISTE DE PATINAGE À ROULETTES), MINI-KARTS ET BATEAUX : 1 F ■ THALASSOTHÉRAPIE TOUTE L'ANNÉE, RENSEIGNEMENTS AU CENTRE DE CURES MARINES, ARCADES DU CASINO, TEL. 84.28.67.

DISTRACTIONS

CASINO OUVERT TOUTE L'ANNÉE : BOULE, ROULETTE, BACCARA, BANQUE OUVERTE, BLACK-JACK, NIGHT-CLUB, BOWLING ■ ROTONDE DE LA PLAGE : DANCING JUILLET ET AOÛT ■ CINÉMAS : CASINO, KURSAAL, REX, ROYAL ■ DISCOTHÈQUES : LA DILIGENCE, COPA-CABANA ■ MAISON DES JEUNES ET DE LA CULTURE.

SPORTS

3 You have received this invitation to a wedding in France.

Philippe et Sylvie

célébreront leur mariage dans la foi en l'église

Sainte-Geneviève de Gouvieux

à 16 heures 30, le 18 septembre

et vous invitent à venir partager leur joie

Philippe

et

Sylvie

After the wedding you write an account, in French, of the day's events. Say what you bought as a present, where the wedding took place, the meal you ate afterwards and any other details you recall about the occasion.

4   While out in the park one day, you found a lost dog. Describe, in French, what you did to find the owner. It turned out to be the pet of a boy or girl who lives next door to your friend in France.

5 While in France, you intend to spend the last week of the holidays with your French friend. Unfortunately there is a hitch in your plans and so you send a telegram.

Write a story, in French, that tells of this unfortunate incident.

6 On another occasion, you are held up by a strike and are forced to send this telegram.

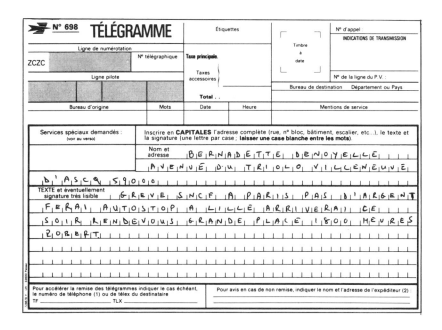

Write an essay, in French, to tell the story of your delay, what happened to you on your journey and how you eventually arrived at your destination.

B Continuing stories

Sometimes you may be asked to continue a story begun in French. Here are some ideas for you to try out.

7 *Un jour vous arrivez en retard pour l'école. Vous êtes parti comme d'habitude, mais en route, quelquechose s'est passé . . . Vous êtes entré dans la salle de classe et le professeur vous a demandé pourquoi. Vous avez répondu: 'Monsieur, je peux tout expliquer . . .'*

8 *Un jour pendant les grandes vacances vous avez décidé d'aller à la campagne pour faire un pique-nique. Malheureusement, vous êtes obligé de retourner de bonne heure. Votre mère est très surprise de vous voir . . . Elle demande: 'Pourquoi es-tu retourné . . . ? Tu es retourné seul.'*

9 *Vous êtes en France chez des amis. Un jour vous offrez de sortir au jardin public avec le chien de votre ami. Mais en route, le chien se sauve . . . Vous ne pouvez pas le trouver. A votre retour, votre ami vous demande ce qui s'est passé. Vous dites: 'Je peux te dire . . .'*

10 *Un jour en France, le téléphone sonne. Quelqu'un vous dit: 'Allô, je suis heureux de vous dire que vous avez gagné le premier prix dans notre concours d'été. Le prix est six cents francs. Voulez-vous nous écrire pour dire ce que vous avez fait de votre argent? Nous publierons l'article dans le prochain numéro de "Salut!".'*

11 You have been on holiday in France. After returning home, you soon receive your photographs back. Here are six photos from the large number you took. They were all taken on the same day while in the Loire Valley.

Write a story suggested by these pictures to describe what you did on that day during your holidays. You may of course add anything else you wish to make it interesting. Write about 100 words in French. (The photos may be used in any order you wish.)

12 While on holiday in Strasbourg, you witness an accident in the *Rue des Grandes Arcades*. A moped rider is hit by a car and injured.

It was raining, and there was a lot of traffic as it was about 9.15 a.m. At the time, you and your friend were in a café at the corner of the street eating *croissants* and enjoying a cup of coffee. You had a good view. The car driver was at fault. You telephoned the ambulance and the police from the café. When they arrive, you are asked to make a statement.

Using the information and some other notes that you made at the time so as not to forget, write, in French, your account of this unfortunate accident.

Cyclomotoriste blessé

Un jeune cyclomotoriste, M. Eric Theret, 19 ans, demeurant à Schiltigheim, avait été blessé le 19 mai dernier à l'issue d'une collision avec un automobiliste, survenue rue des Grandes-Arcades vers 19 h 40.

Afin de déterminer les circonstances exactes de l'accrochage, le service des accidents du commissariat central lance un appel à temoins (tél. 88 32 99 08).

constat amiable d'accident automobile

Ne constitue pas une reconnaissance de responsabilité, mais un relevé des identités et des faits, servant à l'accélération du règlement

à signer obligatoirement par les DEUX conducteurs

1. date de l'accident	heure	2. lieu (pays, n° dépt. localité)	3. blessé(s) même léger(s)
10 08 86	9H15	FRANCE 67 STRASBOURG	non ☐ oui ☒ *

4. dégâts matériels autres qu'aux véhicules A et B	5. témoins noms, adresses et tél. (à souligner s'il s'agit d'un passager de A ou B)
non ☐ oui ☐ *	

véhicule A

6. assuré souscripteur (voir attest. d'assur.)
Nom (majusc.) LAGACHE
Prénom PAUL
Adresse (rue et n°) 26 RUE DU RHIN
Localité (et c. postal) 67000 STRASBOURG
N° tél. (de 9 h. à 17 h.) 19-16-31
L'Assuré peut-il récupérer la T.V.A. afférente au véhicule? non ☒ oui ☐

7. véhicule
Marque, type RENAULT 5
N° d'immatr. (ou de moteur) 1394 RX 67

8. sté d'assurance
GAN
N° de contrat 143 X 19421
Agence (ou bureau ou courtier) STRASBOURG
N° de carte verte _____
(Pour les étrangers)
Attest. ou carte verte } valable jusqu'au 31-12-86
Les dégâts matériels du véhicule sont-ils assurés? non ☐ oui ☒

9. conducteur (voir permis de conduire)
Nom (majusc.) LAGACHE
Prénom PAUL
Adresse 26 RUE DU RHIN
Permis de conduire n° 143219 HB
catégorie (A, B, ...) B délivré par Préfect ure de Strasbourg le 7·9·84
permis valable du _____ au _____
(Pour les catégories C, C1, D, E, F et les taxis)

10. Indiquer par une flèche (→) le point de choc initial

11. dégâts apparents
PARE CHOC
PHARE

14. observations _____

12. circonstances

Mettre une croix (x) dans chacune des cases utiles pour préciser le croquis.

1	en stationnement	1
2	quittait un stationnement	2
3	prenait un stationnement	3
4	sortait d'un parking, d'un lieu privé, d'un chemin de terre	4
5	s'engageait dans un parking, un lieu privé, un chemin de terre	5
6	s'engageait sur une place à sens giratoire	6
7	roulait sur une place à sens giratoire	7
8	heurtait l'arrière de l'autre véhicule qui roulait dans le même sens et sur la même file	8
9	roulait dans le même sens et sur une file différente	9
10	changeait de file	10
11	doublait	11
12	virait à droite	12
X 13	virait à gauche	13
14	reculait	14
15	empiétait sur la partie de chaussée réservée à la circulation en sens inverse	15
16	venait de droite (dans un carrefour)	16
X 17	n'avait pas observé un signal de priorité	17

◀ indiquer le nombre de cases marquées d'une croix ▶

2 ☐

13. croquis de l'accident

Préciser : 1. le tracé des voies - 2. la direction (par des flèches) des véhicules A, B - 3. leur position au moment du choc - 4. les signaux routiers - 5. le nom des rues (ou routes).

← RUE GUTENBERG

A.

Rue des GRANDES ARCADES

15. signature des conducteurs

A J Lagache   B A Givry

véhicule B

6. assuré souscripteur (voir attest. d'assur.)
Nom (majusc.) GIVRY
Prénom ANDRE
Adresse (rue et n°) 2, RUE PAUL FORT
Localité (et c. postal) 67000 STRASBOURG
N° tél. (de 9 h. à 17 h.) —
L'Assuré peut-il récupérer la T.V.A. afférente au véhicule? non ☒ oui ☐

7. véhicule
Marque, type MOBYLETTE 50cc
N° d'immatr. (ou de moteur) 1341 HY 67

8. sté d'assurance
SOCIETE MUTUELLE
N° de contrat 36192 WW 49
Agence (ou bureau ou courtier) STRASBOURG
N° de carte verte _____
(Pour les étrangers)
Attest. ou carte verte } valable jusqu'au 4-1-87
Les dégâts matériels du véhicule sont-ils assurés? non ☐ oui ☒

9. conducteur (voir permis de conduire)
Nom (majusc.) GIVRY
Prénom ANDRE
Adresse 2 RUE PAUL FORT
Permis de conduire n° 42916 COP
catégorie (A, B, ...) _____ délivré par Préfect ure du Rhin le 3.8.86
permis valable du _____ au _____
(Pour les catégories C, C1, D, E, F et les taxis)

10. Indiquer par une flèche (→) le point de choc initial

11. dégâts apparents
ROUE AVANT

14. observations _____

---

* En cas de blessures ou en cas de dégâts matériels autres qu'aux véhicules A et B, relever les indications d'identité, d'adresse, etc.

Ne rien modifier au constat après les signatures et la séparation des exemplaires des 2 conducteurs.

Voir déclaration de l'Assuré au verso ➡

101

13 When you come back from your holiday in France you empty your case and find all sorts of papers, adverts, tickets and bills at the bottom. They remind you of the good time that you had one day on a trip to La Rochelle.

Using these souvenirs, write about 100 words in French to tell the story of your day there. You need not use every item, and you may think of other things you did. Your story could be used as an item in your school magazine in the new term!

ministère de la culture
caisse nationale
des monuments historiques et des sites
droit d'entrée

la Rochelle
Saint-Nicolas/ Lanterne
plein tarif 24 F
A 001708

BILLET
JUMELE
A conserver
pour être présenté
à toute réquisition

PHARMACIENS
Mme DELABROSSE - 17, rue de Blois.
M. CHOLLET - 30, rue Nationale.
PHARMACIE de la Verrerie .
M. LOMPREZ - quai Général-de-Gaulle.
Mme CHARTON - 68, rue de la Concorde.

SNCF
Départ POITIERS
Arrivée LA ROCHELLE VILLE
Utilisable DU 27.08.86 AU 26.10.86
POUR L'ALLER ET LE RETOUR
*147/*149
BS22 055836
POITIERS
27-8-86 09
50731083
7016 0010 50731083

Pour être valable,
ce billet doit être composté
lors de l'accès au train Billet
Via
Prix
Classe
PT 00 001 000 0
F***142,00 A

A la Discothèque **LE VILLAGE**

vous y trouverez ...
★ 3 Pistes de Danse
★ 2 Programmes de Musique
★ 2 Disc-Jockeys
★ 4 Bars
★ 1 Salle de Jeux
★ 1 Piscine et la Vidéo
★ et 1 Équipe sympathique
    pour vous distraire.

---- **TARIFS** ----
Jeudi, Vendredi, Dimanche
CONSOMMATION
à partir de .... 10 francs
Alcool en 2 cl . 15 francs

Samedi
ENTRÉE
avec Consommation 60 frs
sans Consommation 30 frs

UNICO
SORIGNY
TEL:26-07-77
VOUS REMERCIE
DE VOTRE VISITE

26-05-86   2

EPICERIE   4,20
FR/LEG   9,30
FR/LEG   3,60
EPICERIE   2,20
S/T   19,30
ESPECE   *19,30*

3733 09:38

La Discothèque

"LE VILLAGE"
85 - THOUARSAIS BOUILDROUX
☎ (51) 00.81.61 - 00.87.21

a le plaisir
de vous présenter
son Calendrier

des FÊTES de L'ÉTÉ 85

LE VILLAGE
MOUILLERON
CEZAIS
A 15 Km de
FONTENAY LE COMTE
VENDÉE
R.C. 72 A 214

A la descente de nos navires, nous nous permettons de vous conseiller
ces bonnes adresses, toutes situées à proximité de notre embarcadère.

LE CRYSTAL
CAFÉ - GLACIER - SALON DE THÉ - PIANO BAR - COCKTAILS

Tous les soirs pianiste   AU PIED DES TOURS
à partir de 21 h 30   Tél. : 41.43.10

Restaurant "LES FLOTS"
Les vieux matins en façade
Son homard grillé
Téléphone : (46) 41.39.51
Place de la Chaine - 17000 LA ROCHE

HOTEL RESTAUR
"LE COLOMBIER"
SERVICE COMPRIS
****

MENU   *44.70
MENU   *44.70
MENU   *62.00
ENTREE   *15.00
ENTREE   *18.00
BAR   *12.00
BAR   *39.50
GAMAY   *31.50
HOTEL   *56.00
HOTEL   *56.00
QT   4
PT DEJ   @12.40
TOTL   *49.60
SERVICE   *429.00
                 2
06-08-85   8:17

PROMENADE EN MER

● EMBARCADÈRE : COURS DES DAMES
● VEDETTES SPÉCIALEMENT AMÉNAGÉES

Croisière de 50 minutes : Vue sur les Iles de Ré, d'Aix et
d'Oléron et sur les ports des Minimes et de La Pallice. L'his-
torique de la Digue Richelieu vous sera conté sur place.

Renseignements : Tél. 46 44 01 12 - 46 27 01 27 - 46 41 64 40
M GUILLOTEAU - 2, rue Le Saphir - 17000 LA ROCHELLE
Mme LE FORMAL - 17, rue Verdière - 17000 LA ROCHELLE

C Writing picture stories

Write a story based on each of the following series of pictures. Each story should be about 100 words, in French. On each occasion imagine that you are one of the people in the story.

14 En vacances

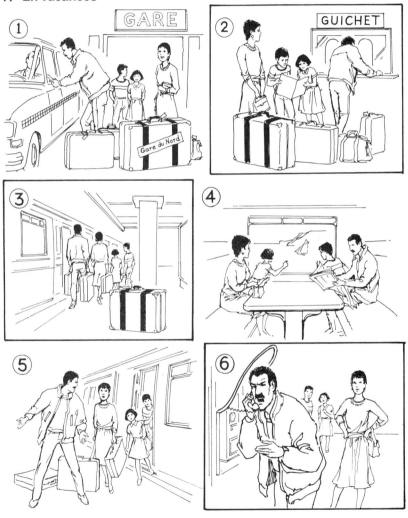

15 Une soirée agréable

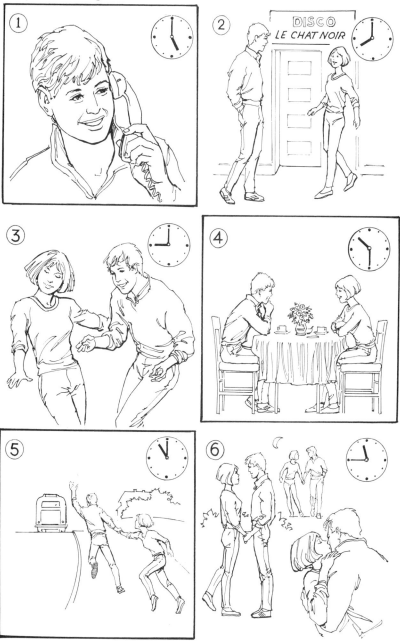

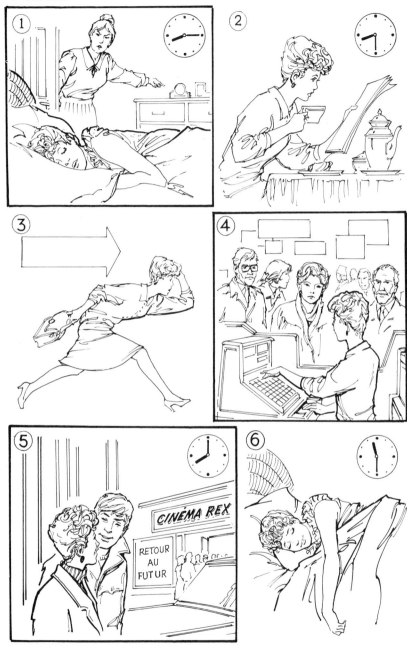

Unit 8 GAMES AND PUZZLES

Learning French should be fun. As well as the serious business of passing examinations which this book has helped you to do, there is still time to use games and puzzles involving writing and using words.

Here are a few ideas. You could even try making up your own puzzles to try on your friends.

1 Look at the following categories:

a) Prénom (Name)	b) Ville (Town)	c) Animal (Animal)	d) Vêtement (Clothing)	e) Aliment (Food)

Go through the alphabet and, for each letter, try to think of a word in French for each category. With the letter c, for example, you could write the following:

a) Claude	b) Calais	c) Chat	d) Chaussette	e) Chou

2 *'Le jeu des dix erreurs'*: This is based on a very popular game that you will find in many newspapers and magazines in France.

Look at the two pictures below and spot the differences. You should be able to find **ten**. Write a list of them in French. For example: *Dans le premier dessin, le père porte des lunettes de soleil.*

Dessin numéro un

Dessin numéro deux

3   Here is another pair of pictures. Try your hand at
    this, again writing your answers in French. Again,
    you should be able to spot **ten** differences.

Dessin numéro un

Dessin numéro deux

There are many books available in France which
feature games. These are sometimes based on TV
games – for example, *Jeux – Des Chiffres et Des
Lettres* and *Télé 7 – Jeux*. You can buy these books in
bookshops and at station kiosks.

4 Make as many French words as possible out of the following long French words:
parapluie; *renseignements*; *chaîne-stéréo*; *correspondance*; *direction*; *électrophone*; *supermarché*; *mathématiques*; *réceptionniste*; *stationnement*.

5 Look at the following picture and write a list, in French, of all the items that begin with the letter p.

6 Have you ever played Kim's game? Of course you have!

Look at the picture below for two minutes, then close your book and write down, in French, all the items you can remember.

Try to remember more than your friends and don't forget to put *le*, *la* or *les* in front of each word.

Topic Index

Topics are listed below in order to refer to the type of writing task involved and to help you refer the tasks to the GCSE syllabuses for your board.

Each unit is referred to as follows:

Accidents
Messages 7
Forms 8
Stories 9, 12

Apologies
Messages 7, 15
Postcards 9
Letters 4, 5, 6

Camping
Lists 15
Messages 13
Formal letters 7

Careers and jobs
Forms 11
Letters 12, 15
Formal letters 11, 12, 13
Pictures 4

113

Messages 10, 11, 18
Postcards 5, 16
Forms 10, 12
Letters 2, 9
Formal letters 14
Stories 1, 2
Pictures 1

Weather
Postcards 1

Youth hostels
Postcards 2, 4